P9-DBW-740

Helen Roberts
Apt. 6-5189 South Street
Halifax, Nova Scotia

# Live
# Youthfully
# Now

by
Russell A. Kemp

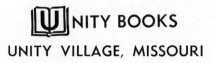

UNITY BOOKS
UNITY VILLAGE, MISSOURI

Copyright 1969 by

Russell A. Kemp

Standard Book Number 87159-232-0

Library of Congress Card Number 79-93890

COVER ILLUSTRATION BY MARGO BLY

UNITY IS A link in the great educational movement inaugurated by Jesus Christ; our objective is to discern the truth in Christianity and prove it. The truth that we teach is not new, neither do we claim special revelations or discovery of new religious principles. Our purpose is to help and teach mankind to use and prove the eternal Truth taught by the Master.—*Charles Fillmore, founder of Unity*

# Contents

# Foreword

*Why This Book Was Written*

Have you ever heard the saying: "We get too soon old, and too late smart"? It voices a feeling that is common to most of us. Does it not seem that about the time we have begun to learn how to live, we also begin to lose the very things that enable us most to enjoy living? How ironical to find that by the time we have at last puzzled out some of the answers to the riddle of existence, we have lost the capacity to benefit from them! Time's greatest taunt is that by the time we acquire the "knowhow" we lose the "go go." Why should we run out of gas by the time we get past all the dusty detours and onto the right road? Does life make sense?

Thomas Kettle once wrote that life was like a meal in a bad restaurant, with time playing the part of an uncivil waiter, who snatches away the dishes before you have had enough of anything. Consider the main dish that life offers, this physical body of ours. According to common belief, our body is built to give us only a fleeting forty or fifty years of satisfactory service.* After that we are headed over the hill. The end is religiously expected at sixty or seventy. To reach eighty is a minor miracle . . . and if we do, we'd better be careful!

---

\* From the viewpoint of an immortal being, forty or fifty years is equivalent to the time it takes us to draw a breath!

9

For it is popularly held that at such an advanced age as eighty, the length of time we have lived has inevitably weakened our physical body, and any unusual exertion might be dangerous. We are told to play safe, just putter around, conserve our strength, rest as much as possible. The name of the game now is "be careful."

This book was written to challenge and contradict such notions as these. I do not accept them as being true or binding, on myself or anyone else.

For many years I have felt intuitively that such commonly accepted beliefs as these were all wrong. I have been deeply interested in the idea of living longer, while also retaining the capacity to live effectively and enjoy life. I do not mean just living to an advanced age. I mean retaining vigor of mind and body regardless of the passing years. I believe we should be capable of enjoying life as long as we live. We should also be able to support ourself and look after ourself in every way as long as we live. We should not ever become a burden to ourself or to others, or to society, regardless of how long we live.

I owe a great deal of my interest in living longer and more effectively to my enthusiasm for metaphysical teachings, particularly to those of Unity School of Christianity, with which I have been associated as a minister for about thirty years. They stress the idea that the true man of God's creating is immortal in mind, and should also have a body that is free from sickness, weakness, old age, or decay. So I have thought deeply, read widely, and studied everything I could find on this absorbing, fascinating subject of living long and living well while being immune to age.

Over the years I have collected news items about people who have defied (sometimes in startling ways) the generally accepted beliefs about age. They have demonstrated that man can be free from sickness and physical weakness far past the proverbial "threescore years and ten." These news items forced me to question even more the popular belief that age necessarily brings decrepitude, for they told of men and women who were ice-skating, roller-skating, dancing, horseback riding, swimming, playing baseball, even running at ages when such things are considered physically impossible.

Then a few years ago my own convictions on the subject received unexpected confirmation from certain authoritative medical circles. Quite simply and definitely, some prominent doctors announced that time of itself had no power to cause the phenomena associated with age in human beings. The changes and deterioration generally ascribed to age, these medical specialists said, are not caused by the accumulation of years; they are a result of the power of the human mind. Our own mind, with its great creative power, has been conditioned to believe that the passing of years inevitably causes us to become feeble and lose our mental and physical powers. As a result, our mind imposes this belief on our body. And this, the doctors declared, not the years themselves, is the real cause of what we have come to know as old age. It is our own deeply-rooted belief that time automatically causes old age, plus changes in our living habits due to this belief, that causes aging.

For instance, we have all been told that at a certain time of life we must reduce our physical activities, curtail our expenditure of energy, and watch out for any physical exertion that might result in harm. We believe these warnings and obey them. We (consciously or unconsciously) slow down, or settle down into less active living.

Also, there is enforced retirement, which usually makes drastic changes in our living habits and suddenly curtails physical activity. The resulting idleness, boredom, and lack of exercise give us more time to worry about our health, time to watch for the bad effects of age which we have been led to expect. It is these things, says the doctors' report, that are mostly to blame for such deterioration. We must stop blaming aging on our years alone.

The reader may at first find this hard to accept. All our life we have been conditioned to believe in what are called the "diseases of the aged." However, in its booklet called "A New Concept of Aging," the American Medical Association says it has been established that there are no "diseases of the aged." To put it another way, there are no diseases specifically resulting from the passage of a certain number of years. "We have no right to assume," the report continues, "that the 'shaky hand, the wobbly step and the narrowing of horizons' are inevitable at any age."

And here we have been believing all along that the accumulation of a certain number of years automatically makes us old! To be sure, we reserved the right to feel old, or to call ourself old, at any period of life. The specter of age begins to haunt us in our youth. Some people consider themselves old at thirty, others at forty. Some may call themselves old wrecks at forty-five, "over the hill" at fifty.

A man may be in good health and secure in his job

at forty, but he can't be sure. A sale of the firm, reorganization resulting in a phasing out of his department or his job, might occur at any time. He thinks to himself: "If I were let out here, could I get another job, or would I be considered too old, because I'm forty? Could I fit in with another firm's retirement or pension plans?" Thoughts like these nag many a man, and add to the stress and strain of business life today.

And yet such thoughts are all based, according to these new concepts of the effects of time, on a mistaken assumption (which some go so far as to call a superstition): namely, that the years we live inevitably work changes in our mind and body, and these finally result in old age.

If we want to remain young as long as we live, we will have to reject and uproot these deeply entrenched beliefs about time and age. We will need to do much more than just read the medical pronouncements that time has no power to age us, and exclaim, "Well, what do you know about that?" There are many sensational ideas competing for our attention in today's ever-accelerating world. Some really serious, determined effort will be required to accomplish what we want. We are going to have to unlearn many things we have learned. We will need to decondition our minds of the belief that time causes aging. This new idea that time has no power of itself to make us old must be accepted in depth before it becomes effective in our physical organism.

And we can help our mind to accept this new idea in the way that produces real results. We can "de-age" ourself. It is the purpose of this book to show you how. It gives you positive, spiritually-oriented information and teaching on this all-important matter. This book will not only teach you, it will help you to think for yourself on the subject.

It will also give you techniques for using your own mind's creative energy, for cooperating with certain subtle but far-reaching forces of nature to renew your vital forces in a way you never thought possible. The gray specter of age that skulks beneath the threshold of most people's waking thoughts can be banished forever. What a relief.

Read the news reports of people who never saw this book but proved just the same that no certain number of years automatically made them old. Read of them playing tennis at seventy-five, swimming in the cold Pacific ocean off California when past eighty, running twenty-five miles just for fun when nearing sixty-five, dancing, roller-skating, even skiing at ages that have been thought of as meaning wheelchairs or rest homes. How can you help being challenged and inspired by their example?

I have to the best of my ability set forth ideas that I myself have used and found helpful in eliminating and escaping from these human race beliefs of age. I have also included some spiritually inspired ideas and disciplines that are helping me at present. I am morally certain they will affect for the better any person who will give them a fair trial.

So, while the devoted scientists and researchers seek to study and isolate the aging process (and more power to them!), you and I, finding aid and inspiration from the higher Power indwelling us, will seek to study and use the "de-aging" process.

We want to find and use for ourself an antidote to the whole tiresomely familiar sequence of life stages, which goes something like this:

First, being very young, feeling unsure and confused, and trying to be older. Then, being a little older, still not knowing what life is all about, and wishing you were grown up. Being grown up at last, but feeling that your precious youth is vanishing. You are still young, even though a certain degree of youth has departed. However, you are enjoying the period between becoming grown up and middle age, which is what we might call youthful maturity. You are still young enough to have pep, but you are mature enough to prize it. This is often the happiest period of life.

After a time you begin to fear the stealthy approach of middle age. Then, having accepted middle age, you begin to fear the coming of old age, all the time feeling just as young inside. Next, old age, with all its boredom, trials, and failing powers . . . while you are still feeling young inside, but unable to express your feeling in your physical body.

There is a way out of all this! It consists in knowing the real truth about yourself as a spiritual-mental-physical being, all in one, and in reality all one. Thus you relate your body to the life force that animates it, not to your birth certificate.

This book gives you definite, provable methods of doing just this. It suggests ways to renovate your senses, renew your body by renewing your mind, restore your enthusiasm for living.

You will be inspired to have a vital interest in life and all that is going on, to live in the present. You will have meaningful things to live for. You will have friends, and you will be needed. You will be strongly motivated to study and learn new, worthwhile things. You will pioneer this new way of living eagerly, not just for yourself, but for all of us!

"It is a long journey" says Curtis W. Reese, "from primitive mystery to modern knowledge, but the journey has been made by man.

"Other and yet greater journeys remain to be made. We are only beginning to catch glimpses of what may yet be achieved."

This book points the way to one of these greater journeys, which has now been revealed to us by modern knowledge confirming ancient insights. There is something greater and finer to be obtained from life than our past experience of precious but fleeting youth imprisoned behind the iron bars of passing years.

This book tells you how you may obtain for yourself youthful and lasting maturity, the new goal and the true goal of life.

# Chapter I

*God Gives Us Life, Not Age*

Is there any power in the mere passage of time to make human beings lose their youth? This may seem like a strange question, since we have always believed that time has power to make us old. But fresh disclosures from modern medical science now cause us to question the validity of this common belief. We all have noticed that some persons seem to defy the passage of the years, and retain youthful vigor and strength at an age when others are feeble and infirm. Why is this?

If time really does have power to cause age and infirmity, why doesn't time affect all people alike? Why can some people remain vigorous and healthy at an age when the majority are resigned to spending the rest of life as semi-invalids?

Consider, for instance, Larry Lewis. On June 25, 1962, the San Francisco News Call Bulletin carried a picture of Larry Lewis and his wife Bessie, who were having a three-way celebration. The occasion marked Larry's ninety-fifth birthday (he was regularly employed as a banquet waiter at the St. Francis Hotel in San Francisco). It was also his wife's sixty-fifth birthday, and their tenth wedding anniversary.

Now it is unusual enough for a man to be regularly employed as a waiter at the age of ninety-five, but the really startling thing about Larry Lewis is that he keeps in condition for his work by running more than six miles around Golden Gate Park every morning!

Time, of course, does not stand still for anybody. On September 11, 1966, the San Francisco Examiner carried this brief item: "Larry Lewis, the 99-year-old St. Francis Hotel waiter, has been widely publicized for his physical prowess. But how can you cease to marvel, as a luncheon group did the other day, when Larry lifted 220-pound Police Sergeant Sam Evjenth. Then the former Houdini partner, who'll be 100 next June, proceeded to match heckle for heckle with Tommy Harris, the town's prime rib."

Does time of itself have power to age the human body? Then why has Larry Lewis escaped? Is he the only one? In the Monterey Peninsula Herald of October 6, 1966, I read that one William Hockenjos, of New Jersey, surrendered his driving license with this comment, "I think it's about time I stopped driving." Mr. Hockenjos, who is ninety-six, never received a summons or had an accident in sixty years behind the wheel. What a pity he felt led to give up driving! Perhaps if he and Larry had gotten together, he might have reconsidered. But even so, think of his accomplishment in driving for over a quarter of a century *beyond the proverbial "threescore-years-and-ten,"* without an accident or citation of any kind! Should not these two men at least make us question the validity of our racial habit of surrendering to the thing called age?

In Porterville, California, according to the San Francisco Examiner, a couple of "youngsters" got into a violent fist fight in the middle of a residential street. Police quickly separated the battlers, Dave

Cheney and W. W. Cisco, and after they had calmed them down, they learned that the two close friends had argued over the outcome of their marbles game. Cheney was 67; Cisco was 76. Youthful high spirits, no doubt!

If most of us surrender to the passing of years and let them make us old, but certain others defy the passage of an even greater number of years, and retain the vigor and enjoyment of life associated with youth, can it be possible that aging is really our own fault? Is the effect that passing years have on our body really an individual matter? Here is what some modern medical scientists have to say upon this point.

After a conference of medical and surgical specialists at the Decourcy Clinic in Cincinnati, some years ago, the following report was issued: "Time is not toxic. All of those who develop a time-neurosis subscribe to the prevalent superstition that time is in some way a poison exerting a mysterious cumulative action . . . time has no effect on human tissues under any conditions . . . vigor does not necessarily vary inversely with the age of an adult. Belief in the effects of time by those who subscribe to such a belief is the thing that acts as a poison."

What startling language! The belief that time is in some way a poison is, they say, a superstition, not a fact. What is a superstition? The dictionary defines it as "an irrational abject attitude of mind toward . . . nature . . . resulting from ignorance."

To put it another way, there is no scientific basis for believing, as most of us do, that the passage of years automatically causes our body to age. If, as these medical men say, "Time has no effect on human tissues under any conditions," then we are allowing a wrong belief to rule us; we are displaying an "irrational, abject attitude of mind . . . resulting from ignorance." It is *belief* in the effects of time that ages us, says this report. And who does the believing concerning this? You and I do it, of course, with the believing power of our own mind. But, they say, it is ignorance of the truth about the passage of time that causes us to cringe in fear before the accumulation of years. We need not surrender to age, if our mind is sufficiently enlightened.

And the good doctors are doing their best to enlighten us. The San Francisco Chronicle of April 16, 1965, carried a report of a hard-hitting speech by a Michigan doctor who, to quote the Chronicle's Dick Hallgren, debunked the so-called infirmities of age before more than four thousand family doctors. The forgetful mind, the doddering gait, the shaky hand—these, said Dr. Frederick C. Swartz of Lansing, are caused by the lack of physical and mental exertion, and not by the passage of time.

"There are no diseases caused by the mere passage of time," he told the doctors assembled in Civic Auditorium. Our present conception of the aging process must be shattered, and our already "brain-washed oldsters" made to see the nature of their ailments. Daily mental and physical exercise practiced with some degree of self-discipline, he said, should raise the life-expectancy figure ten years in one generation.

He spoke of the fatal concept that debilities come with age, and that at sixty-five one is "over the hill." If accepted, this condemns one to a period of ever-narrowing horizons, until the final sparks of living are the psychoneurotic concerns with the workings of his own body. Dr. Swartz, an internist who spent four years with the Mayo Clinic, is over sixty, but lean, vigorous and fit-looking.

In his speech and also in an interview, Dr. Swartz stressed the new concept that time is a measure, not a force. Aging, although it represents an accumulation of time units, is also a measure, not a force. He was not concerned with just prolonging life, but with enhancing and deepening it. The "mere consumption of oxygen," he said, is not enough. The question is, what are we doing with this lifegiving stuff?

Daily exercise, the doctor declared, is imperative. By exercise he did not mean golf, bowling, or housework, because most people do not exert themselves enough in these endeavors. Walking is fine exercise, if we walk energetically, but not if we just shuffle along. As for the forgetfulness and confused mental conditions associated with age, he believes that they result largely from lack of attention and failure to concentrate, also from loss of motivation. But this is preventable if we encourage some habits of study learned in school. Serious reading and thinking should be a part of one's daily life.

If we do not do these things, the doctor said, the result is a narrowing of our mental horizons, to the point where we are no longer interested in ideas, and we spend our time talking about the various aches and pains in our body. He had many patients who took up new endeavors, such as painting, literature, and science, well into their seventies and eighties.

Dr. Swartz also said that "Retirement by the clock is totally untenable from the physician's standpoint." The situation varies considerably from industry to industry, but when individuals have grown with the years, retirement is a waste of human resources. Often, he said, it reverses everything physicians attempt—that is, the preservation of life— and takes away a man's reasons for living.

It is plain that there are medical scientists of our time who not only approve of man's eternal dream of finding some means of overcoming age and regaining youth, but who are busy investigating and studying ways and means of making this dream a reality. They urge us to realize that we must correct our beliefs about years being the cause of aging. This is fundamental.

For many years now, metaphysical schools such as Unity have taught that old age was the result of a false belief about oneself. Yet most religious people believe age to be a law of God, and the 90th Psalm is quoted to support this view. But this Psalm, which reads:

"The years of our life are threescore and ten,
     or even by reason of strength fourscore;
yet their span is but toil and trouble; . . ."

was written by a man who lived to be one hundred and twenty years old! Not only that, but the Scriptures say of Moses, who wrote this Psalm: "Moses was a hundred and twenty years old when he died; his eye was not dim nor his natural force abated." There is no evidence that Moses suffered any loss of strength, either bodily or mentally, from living half a century beyond "threescore and ten."

Caleb, one of the spies sent by Moses into the Promised Land, was eager to embark on the conquest of it when the spies returned with their report, but he and Joshua were overruled by the fears of the others. Caleb spent forty-five years in the wilderness, and at the age of eighty-five, five years past the Psalm's limit of life, Caleb declared: "Lo, I am this day eighty-five years old. I am still as strong to this day as I was in the day that Moses sent me; my strength now is as my strength was then, for war, and for going and coming." Think of that! A man of eighty-five, who according to the 90th Psalm should be as good as dead, was as strong as he had been at forty. He was still able to engage in the fierce hand-to-hand combat of war customary at that time. No shaking hand or doddering gait for him!

Joshua, the great military leader who succeeded Moses and led the children of Israel into the Promised Land, did not concede to old age until he was well over a hundred years old. He died at one hundred and ten, thirty years beyond Moses' time limit. But did Moses really mean that God had set a limit on man's life, of seventy or eighty years? Or did he imply that man's span of seventy or eighty years was short because of man's sins? Here is the Moffatt translation of part of the 90th Psalm:

"thou dost expose our sins
    and layest our guilty secrets bare:
our days droop under thy displeasure,
    our life is over like a sigh.
Our life is seventy years at most,
    or eighty at the best; . . .
Yet who weighs the full weight
    of thy displeasure?
Which of us dreads thine anger?
Oh teach us so to count our days,
    that we may take it to heart."

Is he not saying: "Teach us to know that the

shortness of our life is due to Your displeasure at our sins; this is why we only live seventy or eighty years at best!" If this interpretation is correct, then a righteous man like Moses would fulfill the natural life span of one hundred and twenty years set down in Genesis . . . which is just what Moses did! May not our modern doctors be supported by these ancient Scriptures when they say that time of itself has no power to age us? It is our belief in the power of time that does the harm.

But superstitions die hard, because they are deeply entrenched in our racial subconscious mind, and everyone of us inherits his share of the racial subconsciousness that believes in aging. Oliver Wendell Holmes said, "We are all tattooed in our cradles with the beliefs of our tribe." It is easy to understand how we get this belief that the passing of time makes us older. Parents are always telling us our age, and every period of life finds us believing that we are getting old.*

A little boy of three experienced his first sunburn. After a few days his nose and face began to peel. His mother saw him looking at himself in the mirror, and heard him lament, "Only three years old, and wearing out already!"

* "I mentioned Alsop's preoccupation with age to a woman who has known him since boyhood. She said, 'When Joe was twenty I was dancing with him one night, and he started looking glum. I asked him what he was thinking about, and he said 'Getting old. It's very sad, and very frightening.' " *Merle Miller, Washington, The World and Joseph Alsop.*

We laugh at his reasoning because it is based on the limited knowledge of a child's experience. But this in turn illustrates what Justice Holmes meant by saying that we are all "tattooed in our cradles" with tribal beliefs. The deep-seated racial belief in wearing out, in getting old, was already showing itself in his thinking.

This same little boy, if he continued to express the inherited belief in the power of time to cause aging, might shake his head in disbelief at the swift passage of time when he became twenty-five years old. He would probably look back at his "vanished youth" at thirty, and think with dread of the cold shadow of forty approaching. At fifty, like most men, he would wish he could "turn back the speedometer." He would feel the first pangs of fear of becoming old, and (consciously or unconsciously) he would begin to accept the notion of being old. The man of seventy, however, thinks of fifty as a youthful age.

Is the man of seventy any more justified in feeling he is worn out than the little boy was at the age of three? There is no exact scientific standard as to what constitutes age. Donald G. Baker, writing in the book "Behind the Dim Unknown," says, "It is a common experience to observe young men who are 'old,' while chronologically older men may appear younger." Dr. John H. Heller, speaking at a conference on geriatric medicine, said: "We suspect that aging is programmed in a genetic clock. By this I mean that every species we know anything about . . . has an average lifetime . . . . These life spans seem fixed; it is as though there were a genetic clock, which at time X, more or less, turned itself off and that is that."

On the other hand, those doctors who hold that time of itself has no power to age the human body, but that it is belief in the aging influence of time that does the harm, might conceivably name this genetic clock "Belief." A belief is an inner, subconscious acceptance of an idea as being true. Belief is a form of faith. And as Jesus said, "According to your faith be it done to you." If we believe in the power of time to age us, we are having faith that it will age us. And it will be done to us according to our faith.

Larry Lewis, still working every day at the age of one hundred and one, running nearly seven miles every morning, lifting a two hundred and twenty pound man for fun, keen-witted and active; Hock-enjos driving his car up to the age of ninety-six; Moses at one hundred and twenty with keen eyes and undiminished faculties; the little boy worrying about wearing out at the age of three . . . all illustrate the power of human belief. And belief is a factor of the mind, isn't it? So we can only talk intelligently about renewing our youth and avoiding old age if we bring the mental factor into our considerations.

So far we have been considering the matter of man and the problem of age from a purely physical standpoint. But this viewpoint is of course far too limited. Man is much more than the physical apparatus through which he functions, though he seems to be only this when we know him according to our sense perceptions. Man is vastly greater, more complex. Alexis Carrel, the great surgeon and biologist, said: "Man is simultaneously a material object, a living being, a focus of mental activities. He appertains to the surface of the earth, as do trees, plants, and animals. But he also belongs to another world, a world which though enclosed within himself, stretches beyond space and time."

So if we are to give a truly intelligent and comprehensive summary of the art of cultivating permanent youthfulness, we shall have to consider man not just as a physical being, who is born, matures, ages, and dies like the animals, but also as the embodiment of a soul, which in turn is the embodiment of a deathless, divine, eternal spirit. Only the consideration of man from this broad and inclusive standpoint can truly answer the perplexing questions that arise concerning his physical means of expression.

Therefore we must discuss this whole problem of aging and its overcoming from the true, more representative viewpoint of man as a threefold being, consisting of spirit, soul, and body. The third chapter deals with the question of time from a nonmaterial viewpoint.

We should begin to cultivate this new scientific viewpoint that time of itself has no power to cause aging. The first step is to use the erasing power of denial.

Here is a simple statement which will serve to erase from your mind the superstitious belief in growing old: *Time of itself has no power to age me.*

If you will fix these nine words in your mind and memory by concentrating your attention on them periodically, they will have a definite effect. Your mind has in itself the power to dissolve any thought or belief it wishes to repudiate. This is called denial. If you will faithfully impress upon your mind this new concept that time of itself has no power to age you, gradually you will find that belief in time as the cause of aging will seem ridiculous to you. You will no longer be governed by it.

Even then, continue to use this statement in connection with the mental exercises and affirmations in succeeding chapters. It is one of the key ideas in this book, and you should make sure you have adopted it as yours. Some people think that concentration upon such a statement, and repetition of it silently or audibly, is childish, and beneath them. But most of the great religions and spiritual disciplines of all time have used this principle of concentration through repetition, and it appears to be the easiest way for the average person to change his thinking on a certain point, and keep it changed.

Remember, the true question is never, "How old are you?" The true question is, "How deeply do you believe in the race thought of age?" Remember, age is a question of time.

Let us fix this idea in our mind also: *God gives us life, not age.* And God does not give us life in little fixed amounts at the moment of birth, not in trickles or dribbles throughout our earthly existence, which finally cease at a time set by some theoretical "genetic clock."

Universal life energy is radiated into us in prodigious, unlimited amounts, continually and eternally. Life, as I conceive of it, is an omnipresent, universal, radioactive creative energy. It never ceases radiating itself in and through all of creation, through all manifest things.

You and I tune in, pick up, embody, and generate this universal life force in our own special organism, which the Creator provides us with at birth. At present, we are aware of this organism only as a physical body. Someday we shall be aware of it as being much more than that. At that time we shall live in a way which entirely transcends not only our present imagination, but even our boldest dreams of what life could be like.

And in the meantime? Well, there is a good deal of "meantime" for us to deal with before that golden age arrives. Yet we must begin the exciting adventure of overcoming the age belief for ourself, here and now.

So let's get with it! Let's get started! The first step is to deny belief in the power of time to age us.

God gives you your life, and the calendar on the wall has no power over God's life. "With the Lord . . . a thousand years [are] as one day."

Start establishing a new concept of that God-given life that is flowing through your body now. Start thinking of it as life that is free from age. Use these key power thoughts:

*Time of itself has no power to age me.*
*God gives me only life, not age.*
*I am alive, Thank God. (A-live means literally "In life").*

# Chapter II

*Scientific Use of Mind Forces*

Water has force. It lifts and floats ships. Air, too, has force. It lifts airplanes. Steam has force. It lifts the lids on boiling pots.

Observing these forces, men studied them and experimented with them, learning how to control and direct them to their own uses. Science formulated laws of physics governing their behavior. Men learned how to cooperate with the laws of physics governing the use of these forces. As a result, we now have enough mastery over certain forces of nature to accomplish miracles of power and flight through space.

Yet compared to the intensive study of the laws of physics, there has been little study of the laws of metaphysics—that is, the laws governing man's relationship to God through his own mind, and how man can direct and control the higher forces of mind. It seems fair to assume that if we were as familiar with the laws of metaphysics as we are with the laws of physics, we could do miracles with our minds, surpassing those we now accomplish by material means.

A number of metaphysical movements have studied the mind of man, and have concluded that mind is the connecting link between the creative power of God and man's personal identity. That is, each one of us is directly related to (and connected with) the great creative forces of the cosmos, through our own mind.* By thinking in certain ways, we can direct, employ, and release beneficent creative forces into our own mind and body.

These forces are governed by definite laws, just as are the forces of nature that we use with such startling results and success in the field of physics. When we understand the mental and spiritual laws governing the use of our mind forces and learn to obey them, we can work miracles in changing our mind and body for the better.

Generally speaking, all modern metaphysical schools of thought use two great principles to employ and direct the creative power of mind. These two modes of mind action are called affirmation and denial. Since this book recommends the use of affirmation and denial, and since the more understandingly we use these two great principles the better our results will be, let us make clear just what they are and what they do.

What is an affirmation? It can be thought of as a way of relating our own mind, through our own consciously directed thinking, to the creative and constructive forces of the universal Mind. In this way we direct and release those universal forces into our own "laboratory of consciousness" to produce certain desired results.

*Affirmation and denial are but the channels through which the self-renewing life principle, or spirit in man, works.*

*"Human thought is an integral part of the universe, of the cosmos."—Lecomte duNouy.

An affirmation is first of all a statement of something which we want to have come true, in our mind or our body or in our life. In order for it to come true, the affirmation must express an idea that is already true of man, somehow or somewhere, or in some way. We cannot successfully affirm any idea that is untrue.

Consider one definition of affirmation: "To affirm anything is to assert positively that it is so, even in the face of contrary appearances." This is true, but only partially true. It misses a vital element of affirmation.

There once was a rather timid student of flying who bothered his instructor with fearful questions. "What would we do if the engine stopped?" asked the student. "We'd just try to start it again," replied the instructor. "But if it wouldn't start?" persisted the student. "We'd have to jump and use our parachutes," said the pilot. "But suppose my parachute didn't open," worried the student. To which the pilot, who was tired of his questions, snapped back, "Oh, just flap your arms and say, 'I'm a dicky bird!' "

Now of course no matter how positively the student asserted that he was a bird in the face of appearances to the contrary that he was not, we know it would neither transform him into a bird, nor enable him to fly by waving his arms. The point is that although he would be asserting something positively in the face of contrary appearances, he would not be making an affirmation. For an affirmation must assert an idea that is already true of God, man, or the universe. And man is man; he is not a bird. He could not save himself by such a statement.

On the other hand, if in an emergency like this he said, "God is my help in every need," he would be making an affirmation, for this statement is spiritually true. (There is at least one case on record of a man who fell thousands of feet from a plane and landed without losing his life.)

Affirmations can contradict appearances and yet be true.

Suppose a young man who has a good home and job with his wealthy father in New York gives them up to become a "hippie" in San Francisco. After a time he finds himself without money, and without a job. He cannot obtain work because of his appearance and mode of living. So he is reduced to begging and living by his wits. Sometimes he is thrown in jail. To all appearances he is in bad straits, for he has no money, no job, and no home.

But suppose that his father in New York still loves him. He has kept the son's former job open for him. He even kept him on salary for two months after he left, as a form of vacation pay, and deposited the money in the bank for him. Although in San Francisco his son is broke and unemployed, in New York he has a good home, money in the bank, and a job, all waiting for him! Which are the real facts about the son: the San Francisco facts, or the New York facts? The facts as known to his father are of course the real facts. The son has only to become aware of them, he has only to get in touch with his father, to cancel out what to him are the grim facts of life as he sees them in San Francisco.

When the son learns about the job and the money which are already his in New York, he will probably say to himself: "I'm not broke. I'm not out of work.

I have a good job and money in the bank in New York. I just have to get in touch with my father and claim them."

In other words, all he really needs is to know the truth about himself, isn't it? The process of becoming aware that he need not be bound by his present circumstances, that he possesses resources which only needed to be claimed, the convincing of himself that in reality he is not broke or unemployed . . . these are startlingly similar to what metaphysicians call affirmation and denial.

In true affirmation and denial we are always affirming something that is true of man as he is when seen from his heavenly Father's viewpoint, and denying what is not true of man from this viewpoint. Although man may see himself as sick, poor, or weak in his own estimation, from the divine standpoint he cannot ever be poor, sick, or weak. These are subjective states of mind which he has come to believe are true of himself, just as the son in San Francisco believes that he is without money and unemployed.

The point is that affirmations and denials enable us to relate ourself to the whole truth about ourself, not just to the partial truths about us that we call our body, or our personality, or our financial condition. We have become so obsessed by these partial truths about ourself that we find it impossible to believe the truth about the whole of us, about ourself as the "whole man" of spirit, soul, and body. That is why we have to use denials to dissolve the wrong, partial beliefs from our minds, and affirmations to build up in ourself a consciousness of the whole truth about ourself. This is the truth that sets us free.

In the foregoing parable, the son in San Francisco

has resources of which he was unaware, but they are all he needs to rescue him. Similarly, a body of evidence is accumulating that you and I and all mankind have vast, unexplored resources and powers in the unknown realms of our own mind and spirit.* In reality, the physical part of us, which we usually consider to be all of us that really counts, is only a tiny part of us. It is just that portion of us that we know by means of our senses.

By employing our mind properly, so as to use in a scientific way the vast unknown powers and resources for living which are already a part of us as God's whole man, we can live in an entirely new and better way. But these resources, and the whole man of us, lie beyond the senses. They are only to be found in the realm of mind and spirit. By believing in them, by learning how to avail ourself of them through right thoughts and words, plus actions, we can bring power and beauty and happiness into our life.

The right use of mind also involves knowing that our mind is related to the forces of nature, and that it has its own constructive and destructive forces, as nature does. In metaphysical mind science, affirmation employs, concentrates, and directs the constructive forces of mind. Denial employs the destructive forces of mind. Perhaps this idea of our own mind exhibiting the same constructive and destructive forces as nature will be quite startling to many.

*"The whole drift of my education goes to persuade me that the world of our present consciousness is only one out of many worlds of consciousness."—*William James.*

We are accustomed to the idea that there are constructive and destructive forces in nature, because
we see them in operation all the time. The constructive forces of nature, for example, produce an apple
on an apple tree. If the fruit is not picked when it
becomes ripe, there is no further use for it, as far as
the tree is concerned. The constructive forces which
produced it, from its beginning in the blossom to its
maturity as a ripe and fragrant fruit, are through
with it. They have done their appointed work, and
there is nothing more for them to do.

So they abandon the apple. It now becomes subject to the disintegrating or nonconstructive forces,
that is, to the destructive forces of nature. "De" as a
prefix means "reversing or undoing of an action,
depriving or ridding of, or freeing from."

A familiar example would be the word *defrost,*
meaning to deprive or rid something of frost, as a
refrigerator, or a windshield. So the destructive
forces of nature are really "deconstructive" forces.
They reverse the constructive action which produced the apple, and start another process, just the
reverse of construction, which we call decay. Thus
the apple will fall to the ground, soften, disintegrate,
and eventually be absorbed into the soil, where its
primal ingredients will once more be available to the
constructive forces, which can use them as a form of
fertilizer for constructing more apples.

When we see the matter in this light, we realize
that the destructive forces of nature are inherently
just as good and beneficial to man as the constructive
forces. But we do not ordinarily think so. We tend to
associate the decay of the apple with loss. We say,
"What a shame that beautiful apple is spoiled!"

From the viewpoint of nature it is not a shame,
merely a logical and beneficial action of the creative
forces. These forces having been used to create an
article for which a need did not develop, it is now
necessary that they be used to "de-create" it, in
order to release the substance embodied in it and
make way for new creation.

Man's mind has two major modes of action, acceptance and rejection, sometimes called the "yes" and
"no" of man's mind. Acceptance, the "yes," is the
creative principle, while rejection, the "no," is the
destructive principle.

Thus our mind, like nature, has two definite major
functions: to create or to decreate. The creative
function of mind employs nature's constructive
forces, and we use it through affirmation. The de-
creative function of mind employs the deconstructive principle of nature, and undoes or decreates
what is no longer needed or serving a useful purpose.
This is the "no" of mind, and we use it through
denial. (Notice the prefix "de" in the word *denial,*
meaning to undo, to reverse, or to dissolve.

"The effect of right words of denial is like
water, for they cleanse, loosen, free, wash
away, and dissolve false appearances. The
effect of right affirmations is to fill in, to fulfill,
to make substantial, to build up, to establish,
and to cause to come into appearance that
which is real and true."—*Annie Rix Militz.*

When we employ an affirmation, in the sense that
the term is used in this book, we are using the constructive forces of our own mind, which are of
course an expression of the constructive forces of
nature, as they operate in and through our own

thinking and feeling. When we use a denial, we are using the deconstructive forces of nature, through our own thoughts and words, to dissolve some established belief or mental structure which we no longer want to be operative in our life.

*Using denial to neutralize a belief.*

For instance, to say with deliberate intent, as suggested at the end of Chapter I, *"Time of itself has no power to age me,"* is to employ the deconstructive forces of nature, which operate on the mental level just as they do on the physical level. When we make this denial with a knowledge of our intention, which is to rid our mind of the belief that the passage of time automatically ages the physical organism, then we set into action the deconstructive forces of mind. They will begin the dissolving of this belief in our mind, and its corresponding fixation in the body cells. If we persist in using the denial, the thought forces which have been embodied in this belief will be loosened and released. Consequently the belief itself will disappear from our mind.

There is no element of magic, hocus-pocus, or so-called wishful thinking in our doing this. We are merely using our own mind's natural powers to deconstruct a belief which we did not personally construct. We just inherited it, along with the whole body of beliefs that we inherited when we entered this human scene at birth.

For example, at one time, when a man was born he automatically inherited a belief that the earth was flat. However, a few of the more intrepid thinkers were somehow moved to question the truth of this particular belief. They dared to challenge it by sailing farther and farther across the sea in search of the hypothetical edge of the world. Of course they never found it. Eventually one returned to his starting point after having sailed around the world, and thus forever disproved the notion that the world was flat. Now we all inherit the belief that the earth is a sphere.

*Mental evolution is still going on.*

This process of challenging erroneous notions which are held in common by the human race is still going on at a furious pace. In fact, the book you are reading and the new ideas it presents are part of this process. This book's purpose is to teach you how to use the constructive and deconstructive powers of your own mind to "defrost" yourself of the erroneous belief that age and decay are inevitable because you have lived a certain number of years. In forward-thinking circles it is now fairly well accepted that this belief is a fallacy. Many, many people are now living far beyond the Biblical threescore and ten, not in a semi-invalid state, but in good health and enjoyment of life. You can do this as well as they can.

*Use your mind forces to stay young!*

Say and believe:
*I understand that life's great creative, youth-giving forces are active in me right now. I am giving them direction with my mind, as I affirm:*
*The joy of God's renewing life is now mine. God's abundant life vivifies and rejuvenates my mind and*

*body. God's abundant life keeps me mentally and
physically young.*

*God in me is an infinite source of radiant joy and
uplifting strength.*

*God's abundant life renews my capacity to enjoy
living.*

Use your mind! Use it scientifically to deconstruct the outmoded beliefs in the power of time to
cause aging. Use it to construct, by means of these
affirmations, new beliefs that will keep you young,
while you enjoy the maturity and fruits of experience.

*I do not live by time. I live by virtue of God's life
force within me, which is timeless and eternal.*

When we consciously declare this, we can see how
we are using the deconstructive forces of our own
mind. We are using them to dissolve the belief that
our life span is governed by time. And in the same
declaration we are employing the constructive forces
of mind to construct, in our own mind, a true idea—
that you live by virtue of God's life force in you,
which knows no time. Having no sense of time, it
cannot age. It might be compared to electrical
energy. Can you conceive of electrical energy getting
old, so long as it is in existence? And electrical
energy is only a pale shadow of the divine life force
that animates your body and mind and soul.

The principle holds true for all the deconstructive
and constructive statements in this book. Indeed the
whole book is, as you read it, either deconstructing
or reconstructing the mental structure of your mind,
wherever it is concerned with length of days and
enjoyment of life.

*More helpful facts about affirmations.*

You should now understand that when you use an affirmation you are not "kidding yourself," nor are you trying to make yourself believe that something is true when it is not true.

*The longing that I feel to be made new is the longing of life to renew me.*

*Life itself feeds and strengthens my desire to be made young.*

*I feel the joy and uplift of working with life to be made new, right now.*

You are not lying when you affirm such statements of spiritual truth, even though they may not be in keeping with what your senses tell you. You are just using the natural constructive forces with which God has endowed you in your own mind, to bring forth onto the physical plane an already existing spiritual reality. You are giving these natural constructive forces direction, concentrating them, giving them a pattern to follow. And the mental energy you employ in doing this will be the substance that your mind will embody in the desired mental structure. If this is too hard to understand right now, just take it on trust, and believe. "Faith is the standing ground of the hopeful, the conviction of unseen facts" (Ferrar Fenton translation).

To take another parallel from nature, is the apple tree lying in the early spring, when it stands bare and apparently lifeless, and yet, by its very bareness, affirms the blossoms of spring and the ripe red fruit of autumn?

Is not the "standing ground" of the bare tree an activity, an intangible pattern of force fields already

at work preparing the leaves and blossoms, though
there is no visible evidence of their presence?

And is not this unseen, intangible activity just as
"real" as—in fact, may it not be a great deal more
"real" and more fundamental in its nature than—the
tangible blossoms and fruit that later on appear? If
the farmer looked at the bare tree and said: "This
tree seems inactive and dead, but I know that it is not
dead. This tree is alive, and it is even now clothing
itself in leaves and blossoms"—can you understand
the sense in which he declared this? If so, you have
grasped the idea of unseen realities and force fields
which are literally "the standing ground of the hopeful, the conviction of unseen facts." And it is these
"unseen facts" that later on will appear as facts to
man's senses.

### Youth is still yours!

Say: *I am releasing and directing youthful enthusiasm, youthful energy, and youthful optimism into
my mind and body, by this thought.*

*My enjoyment of life is not governed by the years
I have lived. Youth is still mine, in my divine potential.*

You are not lying when you affirm your possession of youth, even though from the physical standpoint your days of youth may be past. You are just
working with the great constructive forces of nature,
and your own hidden, divine potential, to bring
forth the "unseen facts" of that real and enduring
youth that is ever present on the inner side of your
being. You are, like the bare tree in spring, setting
the invisible forces of nature and of Spirit into opera-

tion, that they may bear fruit, according to what you affirm and envision.

You are not telling an untruth when you affirm to be a fact something which is an unseen fact in your own soul. There are physical facts, and there are also soul facts. Soul facts are real and true. They outrank facts on the physical plane. The youth you affirm to be yours *is already yours,* as a spiritual possession. In order to enjoy it as an actual physical experience, you have to process it through the constructive forces of your own mind. Your body, which is always the obedient mirror of your mind, will outwardly display the youth you are affirming as soon as your subconscious acceptance of it is complete.

You can of course hasten the mental processing and enjoy the fruits of your affirming by actively believing that the whole process is completed. This is the way God's wonderful Law works, as was so clearly stated by Jesus. "Whatever you ask in prayer, believe that you receive it, and you will."

So deny the appearance of age. Affirm youth to be yours now. Say: *I deny the race belief and appearance of age. I speed the word of youth to every part of my being, now.*

Actively believe, mentally enter into, and *picture as yours already,* the desired youthfulness you are affirming. Then relax, and rest in a sense of peace, while your body organization accepts and translates your desire into physical form. This is *believing in depth* that you have received.

*Deny and affirm. Use two-way mind action.*

Here you have been given a way of employing the

two great modes of mind action, the constructive and the deconstructive. Nature needs and uses both of these principles in its ceaseless activity. We too need to use both of them in the conscious application of our creative mind forces. By using them with understanding, we can remake ourself, and ultimately remake our world as well.

By such right use of our creative mind power, we can regain that joyous feeling we had in youth: that our life is still ahead of us, and we can make of it what we will. Get the feeling that you are taking hold of your life right now. You can still determine what you are going to be, and what your life is going to be. This was one of the greatest joys of youth . . . and you have not really lost it. The years have not robbed you of it. Life has been treasuring it, keeping it in store for you, until you grew spiritually aware enough to reclaim it as yours. Claim it now!

When you grasp the fact that God has endowed you with these great natural creative forces, which are just as active, just as creative and powerful at any time of life as they are in youth, and that you can scientifically direct and control them with your own mind, you are that moment, for all practical purposes, reborn. It is no exaggeration to say that by learning to use our mind forces scientifically, and to work in close cooperation with the surge and spring of God's bountiful life within us, we can remake ourself, and ultimately remake our own world as well.

*I am made new, restored and rejuvenated by the natural constructive forces of my own mind and body. I am grateful to God, who makes this possible.*

*I use my new life and energy with wisdom and*

*discretion, to enjoy youthful maturity, now and forever. Amen.*

This method of directing and employing the forces of man's mind was long the exclusive possession of secret brotherhoods. But it was rediscovered and made available to the world on a wide scale, nearly a century ago, here in the United States. The incredible thing is that so few people today know anything about it, and many reject it as some form of hocus-pocus, or to use the time honored cliché, "wishful thinking."

As someone wittily said, "Light travels with remarkable speed, until it encounters the human mind." But surely this is not true of your mind, is it? Never let it be said that your mind is closed to new ideas, with the blinds of habit thinking or religious prejudice or superstition tightly drawn.

New ideas are "windows of the soul." As Ella Wheeler Wilcox wrote: "Let there be many windows in your soul, that all the glories of the universe may beautify it."

May these ideas about the scientific use of mind forces add new and beautiful "picture windows" to your soul, and help you glorify and beautify your body with that youthful maturity that God planned for you to enjoy.

## Keep Young with the News

November 10, 1967. Happy birthday! It's Armand Schaub time again. This means he's throwing his annual birthday party tomorrow at the Del Monte Gardens in Monterey. Armand will delight the attending children with his antics on roller

skates. Each year the redoubtable Mr. Schaub wrings
something a little bit more difficult out of his skates
to tickle his enthusiastic audiences. All this would be
highly routine except that the birthday Armand is
celebrating is his 78th. Go to it, you young old
timer!

November 24, 1967: In Rio Oso, California, J. H.
Biedler and his wife celebrated Thanksgiving and
their 74th wedding anniversary. "Mother makes a
wonderful oyster dressing, and I'm going to cook the
bird," remarked Mr. Biedler. The Biedlers were
married in Minnesota in 1893, moving to California
when the packinghouse executive retired. Mr.
Biedler and his wife are both 93, and he still
possesses a valid driver's license, which he uses.

July 26, 1967: In Williamstown, Massachusetts,
one academic critic finds Herman Haskins to be a
"new, young talent." His watercolors are "filled
with the verve of your own youth," the critics say.
    Haskins, a retired meatcutter from North Adams,
is 80. He began painting at 78 in a primitive style
similar to that of the late Grandma Moses. He has
completed fifty paintings thus far, all scenes he
remembers from his life in western Massachusetts.

May 4, 1968: A 53-year-old woman, unconscious
in a flaming bed, was rescued by her 79-year-old
mother, who carried her daughter fifteen feet to
safety. The mother was only slightly injured.

February 1, 1967: Charles P. Wiekel, regional
representative of the new Administration on Aging,

with offices at San Francisco, told the Seaside (California) Rotarians, "The key to successful retirement is to remain physically and mentally active." Wiekel said there are some optimistic experts who predict that within thirty-three years (end of the century), man may live forever. He said that a British authority on the subject had recently declared on a television program, "By the year 2000, one may have to seek permission to die."

April 28, 1968: In a talk at the symposium marking the one hundredth anniversary of the University of California, Dr. Russell V. Lee, founder of the Palo Alto Medical Clinic and the Palo Alto Medical Research Foundation, said, "The potentialities of a full rich life after 65, and even after 80, are greater than ever believed or hoped." Prevention of senility, he said, lies in activity, but not in competitive activity.

"Society and the individual himself must plan for the years after 65, which can be the richest," said Dr. Lee, 72, who "retired" five years ago. "Aging is a state of mind, and not chronology."

He said the post-65 generation can have more fun than ever before, by working on the "decorative side" of the social structure. "They can make things beautiful, plant trees, work in the arts and literature, even work with children," said Dr. Lee.

# Chapter III

*How to Make Time Serve You*

What is this thing called time, which we believe has such power to produce age in our physical make-up? We know of course what it is from the standpoint of our visual sense. Time is measured by the movement of the hands upon a chronometer, clock, or watch. We observe the position of the hands on the face of the timepiece, and we say it is such-and-such a time.

The movement of the clock hands, in turn, is produced by the clock's mechanism, which is delicately adjusted to coincide with the time consumed by the passage of the sun across the sky during the day, and during its absence at night. Time adjusted to the passage of the sun is called sun time. There are other kinds of time. Astronomers in specially equipped observatories calculate time not only from the position of the sun, but also from the earth's position with reference to certain stars.

Extremely delicate measurements have to be made and mathematically computed from observation of the moon, stars, and planets, in order to coordinate the information gained from these sources and calculate what is called "Greenwich time." Greenwich time is defined as "mean solar time of the meridian at Greenwich Observatory at Greenwich, England," and is used as the basis for standard time throughout most of the world.

This "mean solar time" is not actually based on the movements of the sun in the sky, but on a hypothetical sun which is used in time reckoning. This is called the "mean sun." There is also "apparent time," which is measured by the real sun. In addition there is sidereal time, measured by the stars. All these have to be combined to produce what we call "the correct time." Little wonder that the chief astronomer of the Royal Observatory in England was quoted in a Unity magazine of many years ago as saying: "There is no such thing as the correct time. We fake it."

At any rate, the thing that stands out in all these definitions of time is this: *time is essentially man-made.* It is based on the movements of the heavenly bodies through space. But these movements are used by men's minds as a means of measuring the duration of any event, or to fix the point when it occurred, with reference to previous events. Time is immensely useful, in fact indispensable in our present existence. It enables us to regulate our life, order our movements, and control traffic. It enters into almost every phase of our everyday life. Without the use of time life would be chaotic, confusion would be disastrous.

Yes, time is necessary; but should we let it control our life to the extent that we do? Should we let this manmade convenience, this hypothetical standard of measurement, determine the length of our life, as we do now? Because the earth makes a trip around the sun in a little more than three hundred and sixty-five days, are we justified in saying that we are therefore a year older? And if we have been on the earth for sixty or seventy of these trips around the sun, should we expect to die because of that? Should we say that we are "a year older," or should we just say happily that we have enjoyed another swing around the sun?

And if we have lived through another circuit of the sun, what difference does that make? Were we not receiving the same vitalizing rays from the sun during the whole trip? Do we receive life force from a clock, or from a calendar on the wall? Do we receive life force even from nature? Or is our life a force, an energy continuously radiated to us from the presence of God, of whom nature is only an effect?

If we believe the Bible, we must believe that our life force is given to us from God. "He himself gives to all men life and breath and every thing. . . . for in him we live and move and have our being." Jesus urged us not to believe that we receive life from a physical father. He said, "And call no man your father on earth, for you have one Father, who is in heaven."

Now if God is our father, if we live and move in God, then *we do not live and move in time,* as we have imagined. Time is just a wonderful convenience that we invented, to serve us and to keep order in our comings and goings. It comes in handy when boiling an egg or catching a plane. But it is, as we have seen, only an invention of the mind of man. It has no actual existence, as a thing or a force or an energy in itself, in the way that light or heat have existence. They are forces, but time is not a force. It is a product of the mind and senses of man; it exists only in the mind of man, as a mental concept, a measurement device.

It might be compared to the mental concept that two and two make four. This too is a measurement, a means of reckoning, but it has no force, no existence of its own. We would never expect a mental concept such as "two and two make four" to exert any force or have any effect on our body. Why then do we expect the mental concept called time to affect our body, and cause deterioration and death?

Time pertains to outward events, to the use of the senses, and to the right use of physical movement in space. It is not related to the inner man, that is, to the part of us that functions in the realm of mind. In our mind, we can have a dream in which the events that occur apparently require the passage of hours or days. But this dream can be experienced in an extremely short period of time, perhaps in seconds.

So the inner man—that is, the man of mind—has a different relation to what is called time than does the flesh-and-blood man. In his mind man can expand time, so that seconds seem like minutes, and minutes seem like hours. How long do a few seconds seem if you are in a hurry, waiting for the car ahead to move after the light turns green?

Or the mind can contract time. How long does an hour seem if you are having a good time with friends? Doesn't it seem more like five minutes?

Our own feelings and reactions can determine how long time seems to us. Hence, in the mind, time does not measure duration, but feeling does. This is an important thing to remember, because we have just established the very way in which the passage of time seems to affect our body.

Our feeling reaction to our observation of this measure called time is a thing of the emotions. And our emotions are forces for good or ill. They are prime factors in bodily states of sickness or health. *So our emotional reaction to the passage of time is a* *force.* It can affect the physical body.*

Let the emotional reaction to the passing of a year be one of sadness and regret; let the passing of a year be connected with a marked emotional reaction of fear, and emotional acceptance of such a concept as "Another year older, another year nearer the grave"—and we can readily see what effect this can have on the body.

Fear casts its cold shadow over the feeling nature. The natural enjoyment of life is lessened. The very cell activity connected with metabolism is affected adversely. One unconsciously begins to look for signs of approaching age and diminishing strength. And what one looks for in this way, one usually finds.

For instance, any unusual exercise or exertion causes stiffness, no matter what one's age is. But a youth does not associate this stiffness with age. He interprets it as a natural phenomenon, caused by unaccustomed use of his muscles. He expects this stiffness to disappear as a result of further use of his muscles in the same way, and it does.

The tendency of a person a little beyond his youth, however, is to attribute this stiffness to age. He may say: "I must be getting old. I feel so stiff and sore." He forgets that he was stiff and sore as a result of unaccustomed exercise when he was sixteen, or eighteen, or twenty-five, or thirty. Young ball players in the prime of their youth are stiff and sore in spring training. But every age compares itself to a

*"We age, not by years, but by events and our emotional reactions to them."—*Arnold A. Hutschnecker; "The Will to Live."*

previous, lesser term of years, and calls itself "old."
Is not this to a great extent a matter of human
thoughts?

We cannot remind ourself too often that there is
more to us than meets the eye. We are not a body
only. We are also a soul and a spirit. And the important thing is that our body, soul, and spirit exist and
function simultaneously, even though they have
different rates of vibration. At one and the same
instant, a human being is functioning as a physical
organism, called a body; a nonphysical organism,
called a soul (that is, a psychic organism); and a non-
psychic organism, called a spirit.

Of the spirit in man, I believe that we know little
or nothing. We are beginning to suspect, perhaps
even to know, a few things about the soul. But
knowledge of the soul has been greatly limited
because the soul has been associated only with the
question of survival after death. The soul has been
connected in popular thinking with ghosts, appari-
tions, spectral manifestations in cheap melodramas.
The very existence of the soul has never been conceded, much less established, by materialistic
science, because the soul is nonphysical.

How could we hope to prove the existence of the
soul by material means? Can that which is nonphysical, nonmaterial, be weighed or measured,
photographed or analyzed? No, if we are to prove
the existence of the soul, we shall have first to prove
by faith that it exists. And this faith will rest upon
logic. Logic shows the necessary presence in us of
some medium other than the body, to record and
preserve the intangible effects of experience upon
the human being.

For example, do we not as a rule have better judgment in mature years, as compared to our best judgment in youth? Then what is this thing called judgment? Is it a property of the body? Is it improved through obtaining a different body structure than one had in youth, when our judgment was not so good? If so, where do these changes in the body occur? Is there any visible evidence in any part of the body that such changes have occurred?

Or is the thing called judgment a product of certain intangible factors such as memory, observation, reasoning, shrewdness, and the ability to use inference and elimination in weighing the factors of making a decision?

Consider also the quality of mind called patience. Is patience a mental and emotional phenomenon, or is it based on body structure or some physical characteristic? We have observed persons of both sexes, of widely different physical characteristics, who displayed marked patience.

One must conclude that good judgment and patience are the products of mental or emotional attitudes; they represent traits of mind, disposition, or character. Therefore they must have their ground of existence in something nonphysical—perhaps in what we vaguely call the personality.

A great deal of our difficulty in living effectively, and coping with the challenging problems life inevitably presents to us, springs from just this habit of identifying ourself exclusively with the flesh, and not with whatever it is that gives life and animation to the flesh. How can we live effectively when we attempt to deal with the whole range of our experience by using only a fraction of our resources?

We would not consider a man very intelligent who covered one eye so he could not see with that eye, plugged one ear so he could not hear with that ear, put his arm in a sling, and tied a ten-pound weight to each foot. He would be severely handicapped. But this is only a suggestion of the extent to which we handicap ourself by depending solely on the limited resources of our intellect and our senses for the knowledge and intelligence we need in daily life.

The mind of man is equipped with such staggering powers and potentialities that at present we do not have the courage even to guess at their existence. But this condition will not be tolerated too much longer by all people. We are entering what might be called the "age of the mind." More and more colleges and universities are beginning to investigate and to study what is called extrasensory perception. That is, they are beginning to try to prove by sensory evidence that man possesses powers beyond his five senses. This is good.

Soon the study of the unseen, intangible, non-physical aspects of man will be considered respectable by educational institutions. This will lead to a great intuitive leap of the intellect in comprehending a series of mental powers far transcending the intellect's scope of performance, right within the mental makeup of every man.

We are witnessing even now the effectual challenging of former mental barriers in many fields of learning. For instance, who would have dreamed of reading at such speeds as four, five, six, or even ten thousand words a minute, as some persons can do now? A fresh approach to ways of reading, aided by modern scientific methods of observation, brought this to pass. Rapid reading is a fact. Young people in some schools are learning to read at these incredible speeds.

What other advances in knowledge await us around the corner? It would appear that since we are entering a new age, the age of mind, at long last we are going to obey the ancient maxim "Know thyself," and really use the mind with which our Creator endowed us. Since we have already enormously expanded the scope of our senses, by the use of instruments that mind has devised, it would seem logical to expect that we shall also enormously expand the scope of our mind, using for that purpose the mind's own hitherto unsuspected powers. Then we shall have real extrasensory perception—not what is now known as ESP, such as experiments in guessing card symbols, or trying to cause motion in matter by purely mental means.

No, this will be true perception beyond the range of the senses, such as witnessing with the inner senses events taking place far away, hearing with the inner ear sounds made at great distances from us, tasting with an inner sense the flavors of nonphysical substances, and so forth. How greatly these will expand the mind of man! How far reaching the effect of such new mental powers will be in human life!

And of course, the effect of greater knowledge of our potential mental powers will at once be observed in a new attitude toward the question of length of life. At present, ideas such as the noneffect of time on the human organism seem highly theoretical, and perhaps absurd to many people. But in the world of the next few years, such ideas will be considered commonplace. Anybody who claims to be intellectually literate will either be aware of them or will actually be using them. But why should we wait for public acceptance of these ideas before using them?

Why not have the thrill of pioneering in this field? It seems highly probable that our great tradition of pioneering will be experienced all over again in the field of mental science. We can again lead the world by pioneering research into the undiscovered country of mind and soul. We shall explore its resources, survey them and develop them in the way we did our natural resources. In other words, we are going to discover, explore, and do research in the mental side of matter.

Even the vastest of physical resources can eventually be depleted or exhausted. But in the field of mind, resources are always unlimited. A mental quality or resource or power is limited only by the belief of our own mind in its existence, and the extent to which we cultivate its proper use. So in entering this new field of mind, we are dealing with what is always virgin territory. The resources of the mind are always virgin in the sense that they can be renewed constantly by their correct use. This means that the new territory, and the abundance awaiting us in the exploration of man's mental and spiritual nature, is so great that it can only be compared to the riches described in such fairy tales as the story of Aladdin's lamp.

There is a well established principle, spoken of in occult and philosophical writings, that everything in the world of the senses has a counterpart in the world of mind and soul. If this be so, then what we call time must have some spiritual idea or reality back of it. What is the spiritual reality of this thing called time? Is it not the exquisite rhythm and order in which the observable activities of the universe take place?

Since we take our time from the sky, literally, through astronomical and mathematical calculations, could we not take what we believe to be the spiritual reality of time also from the sky? That is, if time is to have another meaning for us besides the useful and convenient one of ordering our movements and measuring events, where better can we look to find this meaning than to the stars and planets which give us the time we already know?

Thought of in this light, we have a vast spiritual "Greenwich observatory" all around us, and even within us. It is the rhythm of the spheres, of the tides, of the sun and moon and stars, which seems also to affect our body at certain times.* We can feel the rhythmic pulsation of our own heart and our own breathing. This rhythm is also an integral part of our health and our life.

Then in our consideration of the factor of time, we should not only deny that time has any power to age our body, but we should also affirm that we are thinking and living in keeping with certain fundamental rhythms that we can observe in all living things.

What are these rhythms? In the simplest terms,

---

*Joseph F. Goodavage, writing in Family Weekly, says: "New York's Upstate Medical Center and Syracuse's V. A. Hospital have discovered the human bio-magnetic field which reacts to the position and phase of the moon, the planets and the sun, as well as distant stars."

they might be spoken of as alternation of work and rest. Next would come the keeping of a balance between work and rest. Then would come the keeping of a balance between output or expenditure of energy, and intake or renewal of energy.

If time has any deeper meaning for us than the convenience of clocks and calendars, that meaning must be its constant reminder that we are closely related to the observable universe. Since our rhythms are a part of its rhythmic movement, we live by the universe and in the universe, and we cannot live apart from the universe.

Just as we now take our time from the order and precision of the heavens, so we should try to take from them something of the vast, serene impersonality, the beauty and peace we see in them. Men have always looked with awe and longing at the stars. "The stars come nightly to the sky," said John Burroughs, in assuring us that our own will always be ours. And looking up into the night, Emerson seemed to hear the stars saying to him, "Why so hot, little man?"

Do not the stars always seem to cool our feverish thoughts? Do they not expand our mental horizon as we gaze at them? Perhaps they are saying: "Take your time! Why are you so rushed, why are you so hurried, so out of breath? Take your time! You are a child of the universe, as we are. And just as we always have plenty of time, so you always have plenty of time. Take your time!"

If you and I are really children of some vaster scheme of things than the world of time clocks and traffic lights, should we be slaves of the clocks and the traffic lights? Should we not put these things in their place, esteem them for their convenience, use them with respect and appreciation, but also at the same time learn to live by far greater, more universal rhythms of beauty and peace? It is the claim of this book that we can learn to do this.

Time does not really age us. Habits of thought concerning time, learned millenniums ago, age us. We can by effort, with persistent care and reeducation of our ideas, change this habit of believing that time automatically causes changes in our body for the worse.

The persistent repetition of this idea—*I do not live by time; I live by God's life force within me, which knows nothing of time*—will gradually change the subconscious habit of belief in time and age. Daily expansion of the thought, by dwelling even for a few moments on nontangible and nontemporal values, such as eternal peace, eternal truth, eternal love, eternal life, will tranquilize our emotions, and give a new frame of reference to our outlook.

If you find yourself feverish with impatience, think of the evening star. Ask yourself: Could impatience, frustration, raging at traffic delays, a perpetual sense of rush and strain, shorten my life?

Ask yourself also: Could patience, poise, calmness, freedom from rush and strain, actually add days and years to my life?

Ask your doctor these questions. (If he charges you money for his answer, you will probably pay more attention to his answer!) But don't you already know the answer? Doesn't your own common sense tell the answer? Of course it does!

Once an incomparably wise and loving Person, seeking to motivate His followers to make use of the great insights into spiritual matters that He had given to them, summed it all up in these words: "If you know these things, blessed are you if you do them." Let me humbly urge you to use these ideas. Why sigh for vanished frontiers? The new frontiers are in the realm of mind, now! There are frontiers within you that will test your mettle, as those of the old West tested your hardy ancestors.

Say to yourself, quietly but deliberately: *I do not live by time. I live by God's life force within me, which knows nothing of time.*

Seek to make this a mental attitude. It will take practice, but everything takes practice. Even growing old takes practice! We start rehearsing for it almost in our cradle. When we are very young we learn that some people are "old," and that some day we shall be like them. This rehearsal for old age continues at an imperceptibly faster and faster tempo, as life goes on. Finally we have mastered the part, and we play it to perfection: aches, pains, disinclination to exercise, mourning the "good old days," and so on. Our make-up job is perfect.

Shouldn't we be able to do just as good a job of rehearsing youth, if we start as soon as possible, and keep at it persistently? Start your rehearsal for permanent youth, youth that endures, youth that is yours, *now.* Mentally take ten years off of your calendar age, right now.

Think back ten years. Recall as vividly as you can how you felt ten years ago, with respect to energy, pep, enthusiasm, and eagerness to live. Start to feel that same degree of life, right now. At first it will be difficult, perhaps. But you can do it if you try.

Form a good, clear idea of looking, feeling, and

acting ten years younger. Rehearse it in your mind.
You are trying out for a part. It means everything to
you. Ten years younger means ten years more of life,
at maximum enjoyment. And this is only a start! If
you could buy, for any sum within your power, a
guarantee of ten years' more life, wouldn't you pay
for it in a hurry?

But these ten years are not going to cost you a
cent . . . only the fun of practicing and thinking as
you want to feel.

You can actually look, feel, and act ten years
younger, just by practicing your denials of time, and
mastering this new attitude in your mind. Remember the key statement from the first chapter: *Time
of itself has no power to age me. God gives us life,
not age. I am alive, thank God.* and the next key
idea: *I do not live by time; I live by God's life force
within me, which knows nothing of time.*

What a miracle these can work in you!

Dr. Robert W. Kleemeier, Washington University
psychologist, gave intelligence tests to persons aged
sixty-five to ninety, over a twelve-year period. He
found no evidence to prove that there is a normal
and steady intellectual decline because of advancing
years. When older people stay healthy and vigorous,
there does not seem to be any decline in their intelligence, Dr. Kleemeier declared.

Noah Piquette of Marinette, Wisconsin, showed
up at city hall to get his 1957 bicycle license, the day
after his younger brother Charles obtained one.
Noah was ninety-two at that time, and Charles was
ninety-one. Nothing like exercise to keep age away!

# Chapter IV

*Instantaneous Renewal*

Every human being who eats, drinks, talks, and walks around on the surface of this world, is within himself also a world. According to some scientists, he is populated by the staggering total of one hundred trillion inhabitants! Our world called Earth, where there is so much talk about a population explosion, has only about three and a half billion inhabitants.

A trillion is a thousand billions of anything. And it is said that each of us has in his individual human body "world" one hundred thousand billion inhabitants: the cells of the body. Cells are to a living thing what population is to the earth.

The cell is the basic structural unit of any living organism. Every organ, every tissue of our body is composed of individual living cells. It is only because of the marvelous provision that our Creator has made for the constant rebirth of these countless little cell inhabitants of our body that we are able to enjoy life and health. We live in our body solely by means of the continual rebirth of our teeming cell population.

Rebirth is a fundamental idea in Christianity. Every true Christian believes that he has been "born again."

Jesus spoke of this aspect of His teaching in the famous interview He gave to Nicodemus. When Jesus said to Nicodemus "Truly, truly, I say to you, unless one is born anew, he cannot see the kingdom of God," Nicodemus was unable to understand. He said: "How can a man be born when he is old? Can he enter a second time into his mother's womb and be born?"

Obviously Nicodemus did not know that he already was participating in this process called rebirth, that it was only because his body cells were continually dying and being reborn that he was alive at all. In the course of the few breaths that it took him to voice his skeptical question to Jesus, literally millions of the tiny inhabitants of his body world died and were born again. They accomplished this by a process called mitosis.

What a fantastic picture our scientists now give us of this world of the microcosm in which our body cells function! Each infinitely small cell is like an entity. It performs with electronic facility feats of chemistry beyond even the imagination of scientific resources to duplicate. It dies, not "daily" as Paul spoke of dying, but (in the case of cells constituting the blood) perhaps ten million times a second. But in the very act of dying, it splits, renews itself by dividing itself at this incredible speed.

A million of anything is very difficult for the human mind to grasp. Yet our body manages to juggle fantastic arithmetical calculations dealing with terms of millions upon millions, and accomplishes this in terms of time so short that they are virtually unmeasurable. It is evident that there must be some quality of intelligence functioning in these body cells which is infinitely faster and more clever than the mind we use in our everyday mental calculations. What we call our conscious mind has nothing to do with the functioning of the body cells, because by comparison it is too slow, too clumsy.

If our conscious mind had to supervise these myriads of bodily activities and functions we would be dead within moments, for its orders would always be too late. Conscious mind thought is incredibly slow and limited in intelligence, compared to the intelligence ruling in the electronic world of the cells. In this cell world there is a power of intelligence, a power of adaptation and self-renewal, a capacity to manufacture required substances and control and distribute them, which is miraculous. Truly the inner world in which the body cells exist is a world of miracles. For many of these miracles, no explanation can as yet be given.

But it is plain that the body does possess power to renew itself by constantly "rebirthing" itself. And it does this automatically. Since it has become known that the cells in the body are all renewed many times over in our lifetime, the question naturally has risen: why then does the physical body change and grow old?

Why should bones become brittle if the cells in these bones are never more than a few years old? Why should joints become stiff, or the elasticity of muscles depart with age, if the cell material of which they are composed is being renewed constantly? What brings about the change from the condition called youth to the condition called age? How can we have blood cells only millionths of a second old, or at the most one hundred and twenty days old, in a man who is forty, sixty, or eighty years old?

How can we have bones, composed of cells variously estimated to be from eighteen months to not more than a few years old, in the body of an individual who is said to be seventy years old? It seems to be a striking contradiction that a body known to have been in existence as a living organism for seventy years on this earth's surface, should be composed of living cells which have been in existence for periods of time varying from milliseconds to hours, or several years. Where can the "age" be?

Here we have a conspicuous contradiction: age composed of youthful material. Man is living in something called "time," which gives him age. He is aware of this thing called time only by the use of his mind. But by what part of his mind? By that part which is shut out of all the really vital activities that give him life, because it is too slow to participate. It is only the conscious phase of his mind, the mind vibrating on the slowest, outer level (therefore the least intelligent phase of his mentality), that is aware of time.

Furthermore, all that is necessary to sustain life and existence in man's physical body functions on the highest level, at such a rate of vibration that time ceases to have any meaning. If blood cells do renew themselves ten million times a second, then do not these cells live virtually out of the time element, as our senses comprehend it?

Although man himself in his inner vital processes lives in a world virtually beyond time, where innate mental and physical processes function possibly beyond the speed of light, man makes himself a slave of time. He believes that this thing called time even has power to cause his death. And of course the crowning irony of it all is that he himself invented time. He needed it as a useful convenience. It was the easiest way for the comparatively slow form of intelligence known as his conscious mind to relate itself to the beautiful order and precision he observed in the universe. Unfortunately he let this convenient creation get out of hand. Like a genie released from a bottle in a fairy tale, it became his master instead of his servant.

So now we have the anomaly of an "old" man, living in an "old" body, which is composed of essentially "young" material. He mourns the swift passing of the years, although these years are only arbitrary mental concepts of the movement of the earth around the lifegiving sun. Neither the earth nor the sun nor the air he breathes seem to show any aging effect because of circling in space!

Does it not seem possible that if man were to stop associating himself (by means of his limited conscious intelligence) with the movements of the earth in space, and associated himself instead with the timeless movements of the world he really inhabits— the world of his own body cells—he might overcome his belief in the power of time to cause old age and death?

Does it seem logical for man to identify himself with the world outside his real being, and give it power over him? Instead, should not he be identifying himself with the actual existent miracles of the world within himself, by virtue of which he lives? Should he not give power to the quality of intelligence in his body cells, which already transcends time and defies time, instead of giving power to changing seasons and a purely mental concept of this earth's travels, called "time"?

Perhaps you are asking: "What possible effect

could this have on the length of his life, even if there
were some practical way for him to identify himself
with the inner world of the cells, rather than with the
outer world in which he lives? And what do you
mean by 'identifying himself' with the outer world,
anyhow?"

Do we really "live" in the outer world at all? We
exist in it, we move around in it, we function in it.
But do we not really "live" where the seat of our life
forces is, where the energy we use in being human
actually is present? Do we not truly live in this great
world of the body populated by these hundred thousand billions of living, intensely active inhabitants?

Perhaps we should say that we live in two worlds,
or two environments. We live in an external environment on the surface of the earth. We live (to a far
greater extent) in an internal environment contained
within the walls of the body, a "sealed-in" world
where miracles are the normal process, where an
incredibly swift and efficient intelligence rules and
directs the minutest details of every action, every
happening. This intelligence is automatic; it operates
with an unerring precision far surpassing that of the
most sophisticated computers. Its calculations deal
with awe-inspiring quantities and numbers, in the
realm of the infinitesimally minute and electroni-
cally activated cell world. Its genius, its artistry, its
mechanical, chemical, and engineering ability are
beyond our imagination; they outdo fairy tales.

Suppose, then, that we could have such a quality
of intelligence at our service, in order to make correct and health-promoting decisions in all matters
involving the well-being of the physical body.
Suppose we could actually learn to live by the un-

erring advice and counsel of such an intelligence (which evidently partakes of the nature of that which we consider divine).

It is well established that the quality and character of our thoughts affect the state of our health; excited, worried, inflamed states of mind do react upon the physical body and produce tension, subconscious anxiety, or fear. And since this superior form of intelligence we are speaking of is always in a state of calm, peaceful, orderly efficiency, then if we let it govern more and more of our thinking and emotions, we might reasonably expect a striking improvement in health, longevity, and general well-being.

What are the practical steps we can take toward doing this? What is meant by "identifying" oneself either with the outer world, or with the inner world of the miraculous intelligence running the body?

To identify oneself is to name oneself, to associate oneself with a certain identity known by its name, physical appearance, and established residence. The latter is important, particularly when we wish to identify ourself for business purposes: we state our name and where we live. This is self-identification as we know it and use it in the outer world.

Now when we seek to identify ourself from the standpoint of the inner man, we name ourself but we do not state the house or apartment number, the street and city as our address. Instead we identify ourself as a citizen of a spiritual kingdom in which we function as a living soul, a free spirit, with an inner identity related to the free forces of the universe. As such we are related to the light of day, to the unlimited atmosphere, to the boundless sky, and to that intangible life force pervading the entire universe.

In *Lessons in Truth,* one of the four basic affirmations is: *"I am Spirit, perfect, holy, harmonious. Nothing can hurt me or make me sick or afraid, for Spirit is God, and God cannot be hurt or sick or afraid. I manifest my real self through this body now."* Many have been the instances of healing that have occurred through the faithful assertion of this statement. It gives us a practical way to identify ourself, not with the outward man of flesh and blood, but with the living, superintelligent, miracle-working power which rules in our inner world. It is the Spirit of God that is the life force animating the countless myriads of tiny cell individuals in our body population.

When we reject the verdict of the limited phase of mentation called conscious mind, with its beliefs in sickness, and appeal to the Superconscious Mind of the living Spirit, then we can actually experience miracles of healing, or reconstruction, in our body. Intellectual knowledge, which believes in the reality and power of matter, is quite limited in its scope. It judges only by the observations of the senses. And the senses are too restricted in their range and reliability to have the last word in such an important matter as the healing of the body.

If you are in earnest about desiring to cultivate this new idea of having your body renewed and your energy and enjoyment of life restored, despite the number of years you have lived, then you must be willing to take some of these ideas on faith and work at them. Do not discuss them with others unless you are sure how they feel about such matters. For the present, go it alone. "He travels fastest who travels alone" is true in the right use of your mental forces. Skepticism, unbelief, criticism, even ridicule may be your experience if you talk about these ideas to the wrong people.

How can you expect anyone to appreciate these principles if they have never studied them, or do not understand them? These are *new* ideas. You are ahead of the crowd. Do not expect the man on the street to know about these things. Above all, do not rush out and try to convert others until you have first proved these ideas to yourself. After people begin to ask you what has happened, what you are doing to look so young, *then* tell them.

To sum up: instantaneous renewal of body tissues goes on constantly. While you read these words, the cell population of your body is dying and being reborn at a speed that defies our imagination. Zoologist N. J. Barrill says, "Self-renewal, whether of body cells or of the mind, is the source of youth, and serves to postpone the end of every man's life."

He also says: "Some of the most vital cells in the body live individually only a very short time. Red blood cells, for instance, live but a few weeks, and are continually being replaced from a source within the bone marrow.* The basal layer of cells in the skin continually proliferates and gives rise to the layers

* Prof. Marcel Bessis, Institute of Cellular Pathology, Paris, says: "Taking the red blood cells of a man as an example, they control a population a hundred times greater than the entire population of the world. This population is renewed every 120 days."

that constantly rub off. All the inner membranes of the body such as the intestines and the lungs are forever being renewed in a similar way. There is a great deal of truth in what Chief Justice Holmes once wrote, that 'We must all be born again, atom by atom, from hour to hour, or perish all at once beyond repair.' "

The important point to remember is that you are a far more intelligent, far more miraculous person than you have ever suspected. This supermind which performs all these miracles of constant rebirth and renewal is really a part of your mind now, but you are probably not aware of it in your ordinary mode of thinking and living.

Think what a piece of work you are! You have a mind in you that is far wiser, more intelligent, better informed than all the scientists and philosophers on earth put together! This mind does as a matter of course things that all of our greatest conscious minds banded together could not do.

By means of this subsurface or unknown mind, what you might call your own inner renewal program is being conducted night and day in the "faster-than-light" world of the body cells. It is by virtue of this incessant renewal of your cell inhabitants that you live at all. Probably none of your body cells is more than a few years old; many may be only millionths of a second old. Doesn't the word *old* lose its meaning when we speak of such fractions of time as millionths of a second? Probably we should stop using the word *old* in connection with anything that is milliseconds in duration, as some of our cells are.

If we want to cultivate youthful maturity, we must stop using the word *old* at all. If it seems absurd (and it surely is) to speak of a baby being six weeks "old"—surely anything that has been living only six weeks is young—then it also seems absurd to speak of a human body, being renewed breath by breath and pulse beat by pulse beat, sometimes at a speed faster than light, as being "old."

If you want to join your own inner renewal program, here is how to go about it: *Instead of thinking about how old you are, start thinking about how "new" you are!*

Think of all the swarming, newly born cell beings that race through your veins and arteries and nerves like the rays of the rising sun race across the horizon in the morning!

No matter how many years you may have lived, no matter how old the family record says you are, there are young cells in you, "young blood" racing through your veins this very instant: one-hundred-and-twenty-day-old blood, four-month-old blood. Don't start arguing about your creaking joints or old bones, or "old" anything. Start thinking about how *new* you are. Think of the young blood in you! Think of the part of you that is forever young because it is forever newly born: your cell world.

Yes, by all means, think *new,* not old. Think new thoughts worthy of those new cells forever being born in you! Because while there is automatic renewal in the world of cells, there is no automatic renewal in the world of the mind. You yourself have to see to it that your mind is renewed.

Try thinking and reasoning in this way: *If the cells of my body are younger than I think, then I must be younger than I have considered myself to be.*

*Therefore to belong to myself, and be true to*

*myself, I must practice thinking of myself as being new and fresh and young.*

I remind myself often: *I am really a life-created, life-renewed, constantly reborn being. I am not just flesh and blood. I am that which animates my flesh and blood, and lives by means of my physical organism. I am what is called the greater Self, invisible to physical eyes, intangible to human hands, yet ruler and director of my teeming inner world.*

*I now identify myself in a new way, as being part of God's universe, governed by God's law, God's wisdom, and God's love. I am learning to live by God's unerring advice and counsel.*

*Every millisecond of the day or night I am constantly being made new by the teeming vigor of the fresh young life of God.*

In Pebble Beach, California, there is a Polar Bear Club whose members, all men and of various ages, plunge into the icy waters of the Pacific on George Washington's birthday. There is another informal swimming club in neighboring Pacific Grove, whose members swim in the icy waters of Monterey Bay all winter long. One of this club's members, Mrs. Decker, was asked to write an article about their custom of swimming all winter. But she declined, saying that sometimes in winter, on bad days when the water was turbulent, her knees stiffened up, and she had to be helped out of the water. She felt this might expose her to ridicule. Since Mrs. Decker is eighty-five, the others didn't think she should be ashamed because her knees stiffened up sometimes while swimming on cold winter days.

# Chapter V

*Habit Can Be a Prison, or a Powerhouse*

What would you think of a man who never went anywhere unless he had been there before? Friends exclaim about the Grand Canyon or the beauties of Yosemite, or the autumn color in New England. But he dismisses their enthusiasm with a weary tolerance. No matter who urges him to visit these places, he knows very well that he will never go, because he has never been to any of them, and he can't go anywhere except some place he has already been.

"But," you say, "this limits his possible experience in a ridiculous way. He had to go to *some* places for the first time, or by his own rules he would have absolutely nowhere to go now. When did he stop going to places he had never been before, and why did he clamp down on life in this absurd way?"

He could not tell you exactly when he reached this strange decision. He thinks it was one day when he suddenly realized that in order to go anywhere except where you are, you have to do two things. First you have to decide to leave where you are, and that implies that you don't like where you are enough to want to stay there. That in turn means that you have been deceived in thinking it was a good place to be. And that in turn means that you aren't as smart as you thought you were, or else how could you make such a mistake?

Now if you aren't as smart as you always thought yourself to be in coming here, how do you know you're not making a mistake right now in leaving here? At least, if you stay where you are, you never risk being accused of making a mistake in coming here in the first place. People will say: "He sure likes it here. Never goes anywhere else. He didn't make a mistake in coming here."

And in case the longing for a little change of scenery does become acute, you can always go somewhere you've already been. This would prove you never made a mistake, either, because if you liked it there enough to go back again, you did right in going there in the first place.

To this man, his reasoning is foolproof. He doesn't know just when he reached these conclusions, but he's satisfied. He never will live anywhere except someplace he has already been, and that proves he is a steady, dependable fellow who knew what he was doing when he did it.

How would you like to live in this way? Wouldn't it be like being in prison? Wouldn't it rob you of one of life's greatest pleasures, the fun of doing something new, seeing something new, going where you'd never been before? Of course it would. The whole story is too far-fetched even to be humorous.

Or is it? Do you and I ever limit our possible life experiences in any way resembling this? Let's see. First of all, we have lived a certain number of years, and we know that we have formed certain ways of thinking, certain ways of living, as a result of these past years, which pretty well make us what we are today. What we call our personality, our character and reputation, these are the product of our total experience as a human being during the years that we have lived. So, as a general rule, the way you and I live today, the way we think, the way we act and react, is likely to be based on habits formed through past experience, far more than we even suspect.

We all have these habit grooves that channel and direct most of our actions. And what we do not usually realize is that most of our actions are caused by our reactions. That is, we tend to act in certain prescribed ways, almost automatically, when any need for decision arises. There is a built-in chain reaction already established, a control mechanism, almost a master pattern, which automatically causes us to react in ways which we say are characteristic of us.

Now when were these controls, these automatic tendencies, established? Previous to the present moment, of course; at some time in the past. They were built in, established imperceptibly, as days, weeks, and even years went on. It is virtually impossible to say that there was any one point in time at which they were suddenly determined. All we know for sure is they are a product of the past. Grooved into the very substance of our brain, and probably also in the gray matter in other parts of our body, they now condition our thinking. They make our actions and reactions and our thinking and emotions fairly predictable by any shrewd observer.

Indeed, a specially trained person could look at us and tell with startling accuracy just how we would react in almost any phase of life experience. We have fixed the fluid stuff of mind into such definite patterns that it is now a part of our very body structure, and can be read by the trained eye. It shows in the shape of our head, the subtle proportions of our face, the angle of our jaws, and the height of our eyebrows. It shows in the whites of our eyes, and the slant of our nose.

Probably ninety percent of what we think and do today is conditioned and predetermined by what we have habitually thought in the past. So the story of the man who would never go anywhere but someplace he had already been is not so much a fable as it is a disconcerting fact. *Most of us never do go anywhere mentally, except where we have already been!*

We act the way we do, because we think the way we do. And we think the way we do because we keep on thinking in the same old way we always have.

And we keep on thinking in the way we always have because it is the easiest, the most comfortable, the least challenging thing to do. Besides, we have the habit! Truly, habit can be a prison. We are prisoners of habit, but we need not be. With a fuller understanding of its nature, we can find that habit is a source from which we draw the power to free ourself from the very thought patterns that now imprison us! God never made the ideal man in us to be a prisoner of his own mentality. We can at any time, by the power of our conscious choice, expressed in deliberately chosen ways of thinking, start a freeing process that will deliver us from these prisons of habit. Many years ago I read the statement that old age comes to present-day man because he has the race habit of indulging in old age. The individual seems to be tied to the past history of the race. To do away with old age, we must break the bonds that hold us to race habits. Both old age and death are just bad habits.

Fortunately there is a way out of this labyrinth, this maze of mental tunnels in which the tiny shuttles of our thoughts continually weave the threads of our destiny tighter and tighter. We can challenge and upset the invisible government of habit. There is a way. But in order to do it, we must understand something more of the way our mind functions.

Psychology tells us that our mind works mostly on the principle of association of ideas. And this in turn involves memory. It is mostly memory that conditions our thinking and makes our reactions to any new idea or experience predictable in advance. The old saying, "Birds of a feather flock together," holds true in the working of the human mind. We tend instinctively to associate ideas with other ideas which we already have, either because they are similar, or because there is some connecting emotional link between them.

To show how this association of ideas works, and how it builds up habit grooves that effectively sidetrack new ideas, or keep us bound to past ways of thought and experience, let us suppose that at some time you had an unpleasant experience with a man named Joe. He got the better of you in a way that left you smarting with anger and thirsting for revenge. But there was nothing you could do about it at the time. You told yourself to forget it. And you tried hard to put the thought of it out of your mind. But it was difficult. Sometimes in the night, if you couldn't sleep, you would go over and over the transaction. Or you would invent situations in which you got the better of Joe, or got even with him for what he had done to you.

After a time, you thought about Joe less and less often. When you did think about him, you didn't seem to feel the same rankling emotions. Time was dulling the edge of memory. Now, perhaps, you can even smile about the whole thing when you remember it. You consider that whole episode a thing of the past. It is gone, forgotten, buried.

That's what you think! Right now where you work there is a fellow employee who seems to you to be a person you just can't trust, or be friends with. He seems agreeable enough. He tries hard to be friendly. And you can't give any real reason for not trusting him, or not responding to his attempts to be friendly. You only know you don't trust him, and you don't want to trust him. But you don't know why.

It is because something about him reminds you subconsciously of Joe. Your subconscious mind, or more accurately, your soul, hasn't forgotten Joe. All the memories, all the hurt feelings connected with him are still alive, but they are filed in the great memory bank of your hidden mind. What is more, because they are painful memories, your soul doesn't like to think about them or relive them. It keeps them suppressed, out of sight. But due to the way the mind works, there are a number of things associated with these memories of Joe. The mind always remembers by the principle of association.

Let's say Joe was fond of caramel candy. Oddly enough, this new man also is fond of caramel candy. Unknown consciously to you, caramel candy is associated in your mind with Joe. That is just one link of association. When you see or smell caramel candy, if the new man offers you some, your subconscious mind instantly associates it with Joe. You hate Joe. You refuse the candy. But you do not consciously know why. You just react. A hidden thought habit has ruled you. Through the principle of association your reaction to your fellow employee today is being affected by buried memories of long ago, totally unconnected with him. But you are not aware of it.

A man I know had an unpleasant experience with another man, who drove a certain make of car. Now, ten years afterward, he does not like that make of car. He listens to the glowing advertisements for this car today but they arouse in him only resistance and prejudice. He would not even think of looking at one in a showroom. By the law of association this car is forever banned in his eyes. Its very name triggers off danger signals in his memory. The highly efficient computerlike brain systems connected with the painful memories of the man who drove that make of car flash into his mind whenever its name is mentioned. His mental attitude is thoroughly conditioned with respect to this make of car. It would take a very great inducement, some extremely powerful motivation (such as a big price cut, or a strong endorsement by a trusted friend), to persuade him even to take a ride in one.

I have gone into this in detail to show how your mind works, how buried memories can prejudice your judgment and condition your thinking without your suspecting it. This principle of association of ideas, and the linking up of memories with other associated ideas, is of supreme importance in connection with cultivating youthfulness.

In Chapter IV we spoke of the incessant, automatic renewal which goes on in the cells of the body. And we said that while renewal is automatic on the physical level, there is no automatic renewal where

the mind is concerned. Mind is a law unto itself.
Mind can make itself stale, it can make itself old, or it
can make itself young. It does this because of its
creativeness, because of its own laws. Or to be more
accurate: Mind can think in a way which is characteristic of age, or it can think in a way which is characteristic of youth. And it can very quickly get accustomed to thinking in either way. The power of our
own mind to condition itself, to form habits of
thinking and reacting and to be bound by these
habits, is absolutely spectacular. But it is also wholly
unsuspected by the average person.

If you want to experience rejuvenation, if you
long to be reborn, to cast off the burden of the years
and feel ten, fifteen, or twenty years younger, you
can do it. But it will involve some determined effort
and mental discipline on your part. There are ways
of using your own mind which will cleanse and
renew your mind, just as the breathing in and breathing out of the breath of life cleanses and restores
your bloodstream.

The buried contents of your mind can also be
renewed, by being gradually brought to light. If then
they are examined by you judiciously, you can
either consciously release them to be forgotten, or
decide that they should be retained. In this way you
can experience rejuvenation of your memory. Such a
renewing of your subconscious memory files will
cause a corresponding feeling of renewal in your
physical organism. It is difficult to express the feeling of lightness and pleasure at the way your mind
works as a result of such renewal.

I knew a man who experienced such a renewal. He
was not even middle-aged, but he really felt old and

stale. Life for him had degenerated into an adventureless routine of eat, work, and sleep, in order that he might keep on eating, working, and sleeping. The sparkle, the lift, was gone from life. He was stale mentally and physically, and he knew it.

Fortunately he knew something of the laws of mind, and he felt that it was both wrong and unnecessary for him to be in this condition. He was sure something could be done about it. In response to his deep desire, and his faith in the power of God to help him escape from this prison of lukewarm living, his own innate intelligence showed him that there was a way to cooperate consciously with the renewing life force within himself. It seemed such a simple way that at first he didn't realize that it was a form of self-analysis.

What was it? He was just to watch his characteristic thoughts and expressions. He was to make a mental note of how long he had been using this or that pet figure of speech. Particularly, he was to ascertain the age of his favorite jokes. How old were they?

His first reaction to this last item was to exclaim, "Why, my mind is an old joke's home!" That pet expression, this often-told joke or favorite wisecrack, certain habitual expressions of disapproval, had been used over and over for years. He resolved to use the cleansing, dissolving action of mind to wash all of them out of his mental life. He determined to refuse expression to any thought or word that was a familiar reaction.

It wasn't easy. Because of the law of association there were well-established habit tracks to these old thoughts. Time after time they occurred to him throughout the day. Then he would use this affirmation: *God's cleansing life renews my mind and frees it from this old thought.* Then he would take care to avoid saying the familiar words, or thinking the well-worn thoughts.

After a time another idea strengthened his determination. He began to reason along these lines: *Birds of a feather flock together. All of these old ideas and expressions are linked up with the idea of oldness. Therefore they are centers of aging influences in my mind. If I can eliminate them from my consciousness I will feel younger and my mind will be renewed.*

It seemed as though a dull gray film had been coating his brain, and now it was being dissolved. His mind seemed to take delight in working more quickly. His mentality became more and more alert. He began to have original thoughts.

Best of all, he did feel younger. It was easier for him to tackle new projects, such as enrolling in an exercise class that toned up his body. He looked for new ways to do familiar things, and tried to cultivate new interests. He talked to people whom he had formerly ignored and sought out new acquaintances. He tried eating foods he had formerly avoided. He read books that challenged his opinions. Although he knew nothing of boating and cared less, he bought magazines on boating and read them. In as many ways as possible he challenged himself to do something different, to change his ways and habits.

And it worked! This man shed so many of his mental years that soon people who were younger in years were saying: "You couldn't possibly remember that. You're much too young!" This gave him considerable quiet amusement. In two years he moved to a larger city, to a better job, and went on from there to still newer and bigger things. Why not? He had cooperated consciously with the urge of the divine creative life force within him, to make "all things new."

Do you really want to be renewed? Why not try this out for yourself? Start right now. Check up on your pet expressions. Suppose you say "I mean" or "You know" or "Like I say" a great deal. Try to remember when you started doing this. Was it a year ago? Five years ago? Ten years ago? How old is your favorite joke? Refuse to tell it again. How many years have you been repeating such things as "Well, I never!" "For goodness sake!" or old-fashioned sayings such as "My stars!"?

And above all, how old are some of your pet grievances? Write them down and *date them*. How long ago did that humiliating experience happen with So-and-so? How many years ago last Christmas did your aunt give you that dirty look? These "old" grievances generate oldness and stiffness and dreary dullness in your mind and body. Weed them out. Throw them out. Deny them expression. Dredge them out, and then dredge new channels for the expression of new ideas and new life in your mind.

Memorize this statement, and affirm it instantly when any old thought tries to think through you: *God's cleansing life renews my mind and frees it from this old thought.* By this means you will actually dissolve and cast out old brain cells and body cells, and build in new cells, to register and embody the new life you have affirmed.

Does it seem preposterous to claim that you can actually change the cells in your body and brain by the words you speak and the thoughts you think? It is not preposterous, but true. Charles Fillmore, who will some day be honored as one of the great spiritual scientists of this age, said, "Thoughts are things. They occupy space in your mind."

He also taught that man's mind has the power either to destroy or to construct. By using the dissolving action of the mind, usually called denial, man can actually break down and cast out from his body the very cells in which any thought has been embodied. By using the constructive action of his mind, called affirmation, man may build into his organism new cells, expressing the character and quality of the thoughts affirmed. This is one of the elementary principles of mental science. By its persistent use man can gradually reconstruct his physical organism.

We can see now a greater meaning in the story of the man who never went anywhere except to some place he had already been. We are that man when we refuse to think any new thoughts, but keep on thinking only the thoughts that are familiar to us. By the simple principle of association of ideas we deepen these established habit grooves, and thus embody the essence of the passing years in our mind. Gradually focal centers of aging influences are formed. Unconsciously the weight of these slows down our mentality. And whatever slows down our mentality tends to depress our life forces, thereby slowing down our body.

Now, please do not deprive yourself of the benefits to be enjoyed from using this simple practice, just because it is simple, or because you are not paying fifty dollars an hour to use it. It is one of those seemingly simple things which in reality

embody a deep spiritual wisdom. The only real existence that past years have is in your memory. For
instance, you cannot consciously remember what
you were doing five years ago today, or ten years ago
today, can you? But if there was any significant emotional reaction to something that happened five
years ago, part of you not only remembers that, but
actually embodies it.

If you are slowing down, if your knees crack when
you bend them, if they are getting stiff, you need to
renew your mind. You may have had your knees for
thirty, forty, fifty, or seventy years, but remember,
the cells in them have been renewed countless times
throughout the years. And they are not really old at
all. The life force in them, the blood coursing
through them, has just been renewed with your
latest breath. So how can they be old? They may
seem to be stiff; that isn't the same as being old. One
can be young in years and yet be stiff. You must
learn to think clearly on these points.

*If you have years, prepare to shed them now!*

It can be done. And since others have done it, you
too can do it. But you must enlist the aid of your
feelings to be successful. Keep painting in your imagination the rewards of practicing these principles and
becoming more youthful in your appearance, in
your actions, in your thinking, and in your work and
recreation. Use your imagination. Instead of daydreaming, or reading your daily paper minutely from
front page to back, take the time really to enter into
the feeling of being ten years younger.

As a child you could always enter wholeheartedly

into pretending that you were something or other. And you have not lost this ability. It is still yours, but you have let it go to sleep by not using it. Bring it back to life, now.

Start pretending, secretly and privately, that you are ten years younger.

All right, now that you are ten years younger, how do you feel? What are you doing, how are you acting, as a result of this? What difference does it make in your appearance?

Use your creative capacity, in the form of playful pretending, to make your goals more realistic, more tangible, to yourself. Bring this idea of becoming younger out of the realm of airy fancy and abstract ideas, and get together with your inner Self to work at it.

Ask yourself: Do I really want to look and feel younger? Do I really believe that I can? Am I interested enough to find out?

It is a fact that determined, enthusiastic effort, directed effort, plus the mental discipline needed actually to do the work, and do the things recommended in this chapter, will make you look and feel younger. How much do you want this? Are you persistent enough to stick with the practice of watching your thoughts and words, and weeding out the old ones, for thirty days? Can you motivate yourself to stay with it until you experience the thrill of success? If you want your life to take on new interest and meaning, if you want to have again that glorious feeling of being in charge of your life that you had at a certain time of youth, then by all means try this out, and see.

There is a familiar saying, "God helps those who

help themselves." Why not help yourself to the spirit
of new life? For instance, there is a dynamic thrill of
new life flashing through all of nature at sunrise. "At
sunrise, every soul is born anew," said Walter Ma-
lone, in his famous poem "Opportunity." Just what
did he mean? Is there actually some mystical or spiritual influence available to man at the moment of
sunrise, which is not to be felt at other times?

Perhaps there is more to this than just a poetic
metaphor. Sunrise is a tingling moment to witness,
and even more to experience, if one is out of doors at
the time. Fishermen, hunters, sailors, farmers, all
those who rise early know the thrill of the rising sun.
If it is spring or summer, the birds wake early; they
sing even before the dawn. But I have observed that
just before the sun appears over the edge of the
earth, everything seems to become still. The birds
stop singing. It is as if a momentary hush is observed,
as if everything is waiting for the first golden seg-
ment of the sun to emerge. The moment it does,
there is a sudden chorus of song, as if all were moved
by a common impulse of happiness. The golden king
of day, radiant in the east, has returned, to shed light
and warmth and cheerfulness to all of us. It causes
something to sing in us, as well as in the birds.

What has this to do with youthfulness? Just this:
At some time, in order to be rejuvenated and have
the energy and strength you want, you may have to
ignore a seeming lack of results from your efforts. It
is natural to encounter a period when doubts assail
you, but it is at such a time that you must persist all
the more. The results that you want are being pre-
pared within you. This is when you can use some
extra inspiration, some real lift and renewal. So why

not try getting up early enough just once to experience a sunrise for yourself?

Now is the time to do something different, to get out of the rut. Your daily paper probably lists the time of sunrise and sunset. Should you ever come to one of those times when you feel discouraged and gloomy, set your alarm clock early enough to get up, be dressed, and get outside somewhere, so that you can not only witness but be a part of this supreme moment, the birth of a new day.

Fill your mind with this thought: *Another day of life renewal for myself and the world is beginning.*

Open yourself to the wonder of it. Try to use each one of your senses. See, hear, smell the wonderful freshness of the air, touch the grass or a tree or a flower. If there is anything you can taste that will recall some moment of youth to you, take it along and nibble on it while you watch. I defy you to be unaffected for the better, if you try this.

What about the end of the day? Hundreds of people watch the sun set, for every one who sees it rise. To some, there is a feeling of gentle melancholy associated with the sunset. Watching the sun drop out of sight and the shadows darken tends to depress them.

But if you know how to observe the sunset, this reaction will never be yours. Always think of sunset as a time when all the flood of energy that has been poured out upon the earth is being absorbed in the peace and the benediction of beauty that you are watching. Mentally become very still, and think of assimilating it. Now is the time appointed for the renewal of your energies by rest, and later, sleep.

Morning always comes. And with it sometimes

comes a much needed flash of insight, some new idea to solve a problem. A beautiful line is engraved beneath one of the murals in the capitol at Denver: "Beyond the sundown lies tomorrow's wisdom." Tomorrow will be a new day, bringing with it new ideas and new energy. "Let the day's own trouble be sufficient for the day," said the Master. We do not fear to let today come to an end, because we can look forward to tomorrow. Another day will come to us in glory, with the rising of the sun.

Some people like to clear up and order their thoughts before sleeping. This is a good time to bless some old memory and erase it from your mind. We may feel it is not right to give up old but cherished memories of loved ones and other days, and we are not called upon to do this. It is probable that we could never erase from our soul things that are dear and meaningful to us. Their essence has become a part of us. We are not required to give up any good thing to go forward spiritually.

We are only required to deny and erase from our memory that which is painful, that which has hurt us or harmed us, that which is bitter or discordant.

Deny and seek to dissolve anything that rankles, anything that has become old or stale or trite. Surely nothing worthwhile can be lost by erasing and forgiving such memories as these.

Quit embalming those past years in the fluid substance of your thoughts. Stop being a prisoner of automatic thinking. Why should you be bound by the dead past? It is only a record. It need not be a force in your life. Use these simple methods, and step out of the prison of habit which is gradually taking more and more command of your life.

The most divine thing about you is *your power of choice.* You can actually choose to think in new and different ways, ways that will give you an appointment with youth every morning, and an appointment with renewal every night. Drill this thought deep into your mind: *I always have a choice of how to think.*

Through your power to choose what kind of thoughts you will think, you can think in ways that will gradually convert the prison of habit into a powerhouse of freedom and newness in mind and body. Make the right choice now. Choose to dwell with enjoyment on declarations like these:

*God's Spirit within me is eternally alive with the life and youth of God. This Spirit is the spirit of youth. The spirit of youth in me, responding to these thoughts, now frees me from all belief in age, because age is unknown to its nature.*

*The spirit of youth in me keeps any part of me from subconsciously preparing for old age or death. No part of me is picturing a previous experience of age or death through established race memories or habits, because I divinely choose that it shall not do this.*

*Using my divine power to choose what I want to experience, I now declare: Any habit tracks of race belief in old age are now erased from my subconscious mind by the intention and spirit of these words. I am now convinced of my spiritual origin and nature. I am now convinced that I can use my own mind to cleanse and renew my mind.*

Say every morning: *I have an appointment with youth this morning. Another day of life renewal for myself and the world is beginning.*

Say every night: *I have an appointment with divine renewal tonight.*

Say often: *Thank God for this marvelous health and enjoyment of living, which my youthful maturity gives to me constantly.*

In 1960 Harriet E. Rowe of Worcester, Massachusetts, at the age of 75, was busy with roller-skating and ice-skating, ballet, modern jazz dancing, and mountain climbing. Eight years before that, Miss Rowe had fractured her ankle in a roller-skating mishap.

She took up ballet dancing after the bone healed, to strengthen her ankle so it would be in shape for mountain climbing. No "three-score-and-ten syndrome" for her!

In 1963, Arthur Reed of Oakland, California, a retired farmer, rode his bicycle to church on Sundays. He was 103 years old. He could remember back to 1865, when a Union soldier gave him a bugle.

Mrs. Edith Dornan of Phoenix, Arizona, asked to be excused from jury duty because she would not be permitted to wear slacks in the courtroom.

She said the slacks were a necessity, because she had trouble riding her motorcycle while wearing a skirt. Mrs. Dornan at that time was 77.

# Chapter VI

## Memory's Golden Door

Memory may well be, as someone once said, the lowest of man's mental powers. Certainly it seems to be a simple instinctive faculty so familiar, so commonplace that we do not consider it to be important in our total scheme of living. But on the other hand the operation of the memory is of such vital significance in the expression of ourself as a living and continuing organism that there could be no recognizable identity, no personality expressed by us, were it not that we possess this function or power called memory.

From earliest childhood, with the gradual dawning of the infant's awareness of itself as a *someone,* a self that has an identity separate from others, the power of memory is the prime operating force which organizes the infant's perception of itself into a bundle, a unit. Later this is the basis of the child's personality.

Much of the earliest action of memory originates in the body. The child quickly develops association memories with pleasure and pain. He learns that crying brings attention. If he howls lustily he will be fed. Feeding is pleasant. It not only stills hunger but is enjoyable in itself. Very quickly there is a learned habit of action centered around the body's memories of pleasure and gratification through being fed. Other memories connected with gratification quickly develop.

The child somehow becomes aware of and familiar with his mother as a person. He can distinguish her from others, and is at ease with her, although frightened by others. Memory must play a part in this. Somehow he must organize impressions of his mother's appearance, or her voice, or her body qualities, perhaps of some intangible radiation from her, in his memory, in order to distinguish her from others. Were it not for his memory, the child would never come to know his mother, or to prefer her attentions to those of others.

Then, too, his memory has to retain his impressions of himself, of the sound of the name by which he is so frequently called, and which he will learn to connect with himself. He learns words that his parents teach him by repetition. Always the memory function of his mind is active, organizing, storing, laying the foundations for his developing sense of being an individual, a self.

Verbal memory is also needed. He learns to connect faces with certain sounds which are names. He develops habits of reaction, as well as reflex actions. Always these habits and learned things are the result of memory. When he learns to walk certain reflexes must be developed as he learns how to balance himself. The body stores these reflexes and thus conserves the accumulated results of trial and error until he gains control of his body and is able to walk.

The faculty of memory is so intimately associated with the various bundles of stored-up information expressed in the child that in one sense his memory is the child. Without it there would be no child, but only some disorganized and chaotic physical efforts to be a living being.

So the question, "Is your memory you?" is not at all fanciful or impractical. While it could not be claimed for a moment that memory constitutes one's personality, it certainly is the cohesive, organizing element responsible for the existence of what we call a personality. No, the memory is not you, any more than your face is you, or your body is you. You are a composite, a unified, coordinated expression of countless activities and intelligences.

And it is by means of your obedient, instantaneous faculty of memory that you have learned to recognize this body, this mind, and the intangible factors constituting your whole organized self, as yourself.

What a mysterious thing memory is! Scientists have learned that by electrically stimulating some brain cells, certain memories apparently stored in these cells can actually be reexperienced. They are not remembered, but relived. The individual experiences the same vivid sensations that he had when the original experience occurred. Memory is not only like a tape recorder and a motion-picture camera, but it can also store smells, tastes, sensations of touch as well. We have not yet invented devices to record and reproduce smells or tastes or the feeling of things touched. But our memory does it constantly.

Is memory a function of the body? Or is it a function of the mind? We would have to say that it partakes of the power of both body and mind. But does memory have still deeper levels than the physical and mental? Is there a still deeper or higher level on which memory functions? Is memory also a power of man's psychic organism? Or is memory and the sense of individuality dependent upon the physical instrument of body cells and the expression of what we call our mind through this body organism?

The question is: does the sense of self, or personal identity, persist after the event called death, when we no longer possess a physical organism? Can the individual, though disembodied, retain his sense of identity and also remember names, persons, and events once familiar to him, though he has no brain cells or physical organism in which they formerly seemed to be stored, subject to recall? This is indeed an important question.

There is a very impressive body of testimony indicating that individuals who no longer are living in a fleshly body can express memory of themselves and also memories of those formerly known to them. Much careful investigation has been conducted. Amazing experiences have been recorded in which persons living in their fleshly bodies have communicated with persons no longer living on this earth. In these experiences the person who was "departed" (as we say) from this life revealed ability to transmit information of certain events that had not yet occurred in the physical world. The "soul" or "spirit" of the deceased person definitely expressed the same power of memory as was expressed during the physical lifetime. Though the person no longer had physical brain cells to tap for memories, he still possessed (and was able to recall) these memories.

One who believes that man exists not only as a flesh organism but also as a psychic organism called a soul, finds in such experiences confirmation of the fact that man has a soul. Or, more correctly, that man *is* a soul. This organization called a soul, while it inhabits the physical body during one's lifetime, can function as an entity without the physical body.

If only we could stop thinking of ourself as a person consisting of a fleshly body, with some sort of vague thing connected with it called a soul! And if we could think of ourself as a living, vital, nonmaterial being which animates and uses this fleshly body, how great an advance in civilized living would be possible!

We would then be able to enlist in our service the superior mental resources of the nonphysical part of us, which functions on a level of intelligence far above the conscious mind. If we could develop our latent ability to use our faculties of seeing, for instance, on the soul level, how wonderful our sight would be! We could see anything, anywhere, on the earth's surface. We could see the spoiled berries at the bottom of the box, underneath the fresh berries at the top. We could read a book without opening it. We could know intuitively, swiftly and surely, so much that we now may not fully grasp with the intellect even after years of study and research.

We would then understand that the faculty of memory is really a faculty of man's soul. Man's memory in its innermost phase has registered, in essence, all the manifold, multifarious experiences his soul has lived, since it first began an individual existence. The soul is the embodied essence of all man's memories of existence.

But this type of memory is infinitely deeper and less accessible than the ordinary memory with which we are familiar. The verbal memory of names, words, faces, facts which works by the principle of association, the body memory by which we learn habits of action, which gives us physical reflexes, instinctive actions, and established skills—these belong to what might be called the outer phase of memory. For convenience, let us call it the outer memory. The verbal memory works by association. We tend to remember things according to our estimate of their importance. We can remember with ease the name of a person whose good will is important to us because he is associated in our mind with some interest of ours, financial or social. It will pay us to remember his name.

In my opinion the inner memory depends mostly on feeling. It records things that once aroused a feeling reaction, whether of love, hate, or fear. It remembers things learned through feeling, things that delight or please. This phase of memory centers in what is called the emotional body. It learns by feeling.

Yet there is a still deeper, or higher, level of memory than these two. Let us call it the "true" memory. It is the divine reality of memory, the highest and truest expression of it. This true memory is not so much a faculty of man's soul as it is of his higher Self, or Spirit. It is but little known. Yet this true memory holds in trust for man the secrets of his divine endowment as a creature created by God, in the image and likeness of God.

Because the divine man, the true idea of man, is the idea of a spiritual being, made by God out of God's own substance and life, then this spiritual idea of man must partake of the divine nature, for there is nothing else for him to partake of. Being divine in essence, in his fundamental nature, he is unconscious of time. Since time as we know it is a product of the senses, experienced by the senses, then time pertains strictly to the material world of form and space.

However, Spirit knows no time. As Peter said, "With the Lord one day is as a thousand years, and a thousand years as one day." I interpret this to mean that God is neither limited by, nor bound by, our human beliefs of time. God is Spirit, and Spirit knows only one time. Since Spirit is perfect now, then there is no need for change, which would involve a process, and a process would require time. Spirit is timeless. Since it is the belief in time that causes man to age, Spirit is ageless. Being ageless, Spirit is neither young nor old, but is changeless perfection of life.

The nearest thing to this changeless perfection of life we human beings can know is the glory of physical youth. It is then that vitality is at its peak, the mind is keen and impressionable, the senses are fresh and a perpetual source of delight, the body is glowing with energy, recuperative power is at its highest.

Our true memory remembers the spiritual essence of all this; it can be said to hold it in trust for us. So we can say that our true memory holds in trust for us the secret of true immortal youth, the glory of existence as it was once imaged for us on the highest level by our Creator.

How can we revive our true memory? We must first believe in it, believe that there is such a thing as a perfect spiritual memory. Second, we must know that our outer memory (by which we now memorize information or names or faces) and our inner memory (by which we remember feelings and emotional experiences) are in reality but phases of our true memory, which includes both of them in itself.

So we begin to establish in our mind the great fact

that our true memory is a divine endowment. Being divine, it partakes of the immortal nature of all spiritual identity. Being divine, it need never fail. One should say earnestly and believingly: *My true memory is a gift of God.* One should affirm this almost endlessly, until he experiences an awakening of his power of remembering.

Since it has been proved by hypnosis that one actually does not forget any experience, and is able, when under hypnosis, to recall vivid details of experiences that are forgotten by the conscious mind, this would seem to support the theory that our memory is already perfect on the subconscious level. If memory is perfect on the subconscious level, what a wider range of powers it must have when operating on the superconscious level! This is our true memory. It can be revived and we can, by persistence, remember that we are truly immortal beings, right now. And, if we are immortal, then "Time shall not wither us, nor the years condemn."

Let us use the energy of our imagination to make this idea more real to us. Picture to yourself a golden door, gleaming with its covering of precious metal, beautifully engraved with designs of a mystic tree, laden with fruits. The colors of the fruits have been worked out with precious stones, such as topaz, carnelian, ruby, sapphire, diamonds. On this door are engraved the words:

IF YOU CAN OPEN THIS DOOR, YOU CAN BE YOUNG FOREVER.

OPEN THIS DOOR, AND ENTER INTO ETERNAL YOUTHFULNESS.

But how does one open this golden door? There is no handle, no knob, no lock, no key. It is perfectly

flush and tight all around; there is not a sign of a
crack into which you could insert a knife blade or
the thinnest wedge. You try to shake it. You pound
on it. It is immovable as solid rock. Obviously if the
door is to be opened, it must be by someone or
something on the inside, not from where you are. If
you could only open it, and walk through into
immortal youthfulness! Then there would be for
you no more age, no more failing powers. No more
getting old, or heavy, or tired or wrinkled. Just to
live at your peak, mentally, physically, and spiritually, forever! But oh, God, how do you open it?

From the inside, of course. But you are outside.
Ah, but you can *think of yourself* being inside, can't
you? Well, what good would that do? Try it and see.

What is it like inside the golden door? Is there
some magic element in the air inside, is it ionized so
that you always feel fresh and vigorous? Does every
breath you draw renew you like a good night's sleep?

What do you see inside? Is there a garden filled
with perfume of flowers? Is there a drinking fountain, whose waters sparkle in the clear golden light
like diamond drops? Are there throngs of youthful-
looking, happy people, all pleasant of face and busily
enjoying each moment? What lies beyond the golden
door? Can you think your way inside? Yes, you can.
In fact, *this is the only way to open the door.* Think
your way inside, and then open the door so that your
flesh and blood and bones can walk in, and you and
your body can enjoy youth together forever.

Since your true memory holds the secret of
youth, then your true memory must be the golden
door. And since you cannot open it from the outside, but have to think your way in, before you can

open the door for your body to join you, then the meaning is that you must think so as to revive your true memory, and make its treasures available to you—the conscious reasoning self of you.

How can you revive your true memory? You must affirm prayerfully that God within is reviving it for you. In addition to affirming faithfully and persistently, *"My true memory is a gift from God,"* you should affirm as well: *"God the faithful and true, the everliving Spirit, is my true memory. It is alive in God now."*

Gradually your true memory will awaken. This does not mean that you will necessarily have any supernatural occurrences. It does mean that your ordinary verbal and reasoning memory will improve. You will find yourself recalling needed facts, names, faces without effort and without error. You will be delighted by the keenness and dependability of your memory. But there is more to come than this. This is merely the first effect of awaking your true memory.

A still greater joy of awakening your true memory is to be able to remember and recall at will anything that is good and necessary for you to recall. Since this power of recall is a faculty of your true memory, and your true memory is a faculty of your divine endowment, it will never fail or pass away.

How distressing it is to see a person still in good health, and otherwise functioning normally, who is unable to recall things which happened a few moments before, although he can remember vividly events of half a century ago. This is one of the pathetic aspects of the race belief in the power of time to cause aging and failing powers. Awaken your true memory, clear your racial subconscious mind function of the belief in age, and your memory need never fail . . . another boon from cultivating permanent youth.

We should also remember that memory thrives on use, and weakens with disuse. We must persistently cultivate this true memory, make use of it, and above all, nourish it. Does this sound strange, to speak of nourishing your memory? Everything that expresses life needs nourishment to sustain its existence. The memory is no exception.

However, the nourishment for your memory is less tangible than food and drink. It consists of such intangible but intensely real things as hope, optimism, enthusiasm, and joy. To nourish the memory, remember the good hopes you cherished, which you may have let languish over the years.

Can you remember one or two of them? Prompt your memory. Don't try to force it, but take an attitude of optimism, a sunny assurance that your memory is unfailing so that this formerly cherished hope will easily be recalled to your conscious remembrance.

Real hope is confident desire for some form of good, coupled with keen anticipation and expectation of receiving it. When your unfailing memory honors your optimistic expectation of recalling this former hope, and presents it once again to your conscious recognition, be glad. Give thanks to your memory, as a valued friend who has done you a great service.

Be enthusiastic about cherishing and reviving this former hope if it is still good and still desirable. Affirm that you are drawing on the infinite capacity for enthusiasm that you have in the spiritual side of your nature.

Remember that hope, optimism, enthusiasm, and joy are like nourishing food for this memory which holds the secret of youth.

Try to believe that this wonderful faculty, your true memory, is as real as the memory with which you are already familiar. A mental faculty such as this seems almost to have an element of personality about it, inasmuch as it responds to recognition and praise just as a person does. So when you start to recognize this true memory by giving your attention and expectation to it, and by making an effort to be hopeful, optimistic, enthusiastic, and joyful about it, your memory will respond just as a person would.

There is probably not a person living who has not at some time made an effort to cultivate the friendship and good will of someone else. Each of us has an instinctive idea of how to go about it. It may require effort for us to treat one of our own mental faculties as though it were a person whose good will we were cultivating. But you would not be reading this unless you had the type of mind that understands what is meant, and is capable of doing it.

If you really want to open that golden door, and find the secret of immortal youthfulness, feed your true memory with youth-giving materials, with hope, optimism, enthusiasm, and joy.

Don't just read this and think: "Isn't that interesting! I must try it sometime." *Sometime is never. Do it now!*

You must work at this. You must take it seriously if you want to be young again.

Do you really want to open that golden door? If your answer is yes, add this affirmation to the other two:

*My true memory is nourished by divine pulsations of hope, optimism, enthusiasm, and joy. I bestow hearty blessings of praise upon this wonderful gift of God. And it responds by serving me more and more.*

## To Stay Young, Keep Moving

At eighty-seven, according to the San Francisco Chronicle, Rudolf Friml, famous composer of operettas, was unwilling to rest on his musical laurels. He was turning to a new form of "highbrow" music, a serious work. Asked why he took up the job of composing in a form which to him was new and unfamiliar, he replied: "My light operas and musical comedies were all right in my younger days. But now I have reached the time to do something more serious. Besides, I enjoy it. The challenge of it is stimulating."

The world-renowned composer, who learned ballet dancing in his student days in Prague, is still youthfully agile and flexible, as he proved by doing gracefully the four basic ballet exercises. He backkicked, dipped, and turned, causing his wife to plead, "Rudolf, please don't overdo it!" How does he remain so youthful? He takes long walks through Sutro Forest and on the beach. On warmer days he takes dips in the ocean.

But "one must not walk like an old man," he declared, hunching his shoulders, bowing his head and shuffling across the room. He then stood erect with head high and walked with quick, stomping steps back across the room. "You see the difference?" he asked.

# Chapter VII

*Renew Your Life Motivation*

Are you enjoying life? You should be, if you want to live a long time at the height of your mental and physical effectiveness. For permanent youthfulness means just this: to be able to live with keen enjoyment of every day and every experience that the day brings. It means having the hopeful, optimistic, "yeasty" feeling of your teens, the natural vitality, the fearlessness and willingness to adventure that is felt in one's twenties, with the happy certainty that one will live forever that we all knew at this period of life.

To remember vividly the time when we felt this way is a powerful incentive to putting forth the necessary mental and physical effort involved in doing the things necessary to regain youthful enjoyment of life. And if we want to slough off the weight of the years, we need plenty of incentive to persist in our endeavors.

There isn't any magical drug, or vitamin pill, or secret combination of words, or six-second exercise that will effortlessly banish the effects of the race belief in time and restore to us the physical condition of youth. We have believed in old age as inevitable for countless centuries. We now have the bad habit of believing in the creeping onslaught of old age, and as the French say, "There is nothing more habit-forming than habit."

The only way to uproot a bad habit is to form a

good habit, which is its opposite. If we really want to
be renewed in mind and body and regain the youthfulness that makes life a joy, we must form new
habits of thinking and new ways of living which will
bring to the surface the spiritual youthfulness imprisoned within the cells and organs of our present
body.

This is not to depreciate the discoveries made by
devoted researchers in the realm of nutrition, the
knowledge of the effect of vitamins on the body and
the role they can fulfill in helping us to keep youthful. Inform yourself in these vital areas of knowledge, by all means. There are many fine books on
these subjects. There is no doubt that a proper
understanding of the part played by nutrition and
the different vitamins, and a willingness to use this
understanding in one's diet, are absolutely necessary
if we wish to attain permanent youthfulness.

Those who are enthusiastic on the subject of
nutrition may insist that "right eating" is all that is
necessary to keep you healthy and young, just as
those who are enthusiastic about the power of mind
will contend that all you need to stay young is to
"know the Truth." Still others are certain that exercise and care of the physical body are enough to
guarantee youthfulness.

My own opinion, after many years of pursuing
knowledge in all of these areas, is that all three are
essential. I believe that a wise combination of diet
and vital foods, spiritual thinking and living, plus
consistent exercise, is required if we are to attain this
"promised land" of perpetual youthfulness. The
object of this book is not only to inform you of what
you need to know, but also to motivate you to do

the things you absolutely *must* do, if you desire to take advantage of the new discoveries in medicine, diet, and mental attitudes concerning youthfulness.

This thing called motivation is so important that we should discuss it before going any further. A motive is any need, any idea, any emotion or desire that causes you to act in response to it. The word *motive* is of course related to the word *motion,* which means "movement." Motivation is your reason for putting forth effort to attain some desire or some goal. But in a better sense, motivation is the art or science of cultivating and sustaining in yourself those feelings and desires that move you to the effort necessary in attaining a chosen goal.

It is vitally important that we know how to motivate ourself to effort and industry in pursuing a chosen objective. Inertia seems to lurk near every ideal, every good desire, ready to pounce on us and ride us like Sinbad's "Old Man of the Sea." Its promptings are tempting; it is easy to succumb to the stealthy infiltration that would cause us to bog down in the pursuit of comfort and ease, the indulgence of well-worn habit tracks of postponement and avoidance of effort. What untold numbers of great dreams have been mired in inertia! How many great ideals have been lost in laziness and dissipated in day-dreams!*

If you are human enough to want to renew your youth, you are also human enough to succumb to the natural inertia of human thinking, and let it reduce your desire to a mere "wanting to want" to be

*Jung speaks of man's greatest passion, "idleness."

renewed. It is easy to read any book like this and get fired up with enthusiasm. It is also so easy to have that enthusiasm fade (and even disappear altogether) when you try to fit new ways of thinking, living, and exercising into your established routine. Inertia, the "stealthy down-drag" of drowsy, mesmerized human thought habits and instinctive reactions which we dignify by the name of "thinking," holds all of us in its grip to an extent we seldom suspect. We can sympathize with the efforts to awaken and clarify the human mind by means of psychedelic drugs, when we see them as an attempt to free the mind from this numbing sleepiness and heaviness, this spell of thick-wittedness that seems to possess us as a species.

However, these drugs, while they may seem to enlarge or expand or liberate the mind, are said by competent medical opinion to be highly dangerous. They numb the faculty of judgment, that priceless quality of control which enables us to discriminate and choose. They make the sober processes of reason, the exercise of effort and industry in self-development, seem boring and repellent. If all one needs to soar into the ultimate expansion of mental powers is a speck of matter, why bother with anything else? Why indeed?

One good reason for not taking these drugs is the testimony of competent observers that the feeling of mental expansion, although it may, for instance, give one the feeling of having great artistic capacity, never leads to any actual artistic accomplishment. The mere enjoyment of the feeling of being able to accomplish great things satisfies the individual, so that he seldom attempts to do anything about it. Or

when he does, his efforts, though they seem master-
ful to him and marvelous, are not equal to what he
accomplished by himself, without the drug. The
point is that the psychedelic drugs disorient the
user's capacity to make sound value judgments, so
that he thinks the work is wonderful and the results
of the drug are wonderful, when in fact the whole
thing is disastrous. According to a medical bulletin
issued by Harvard University, the effect of LSD was
so detrimental that a student taking even one "trip"
should not try to make any important value judgment for six months afterward.

Fortunately there are infinitely better ways of
waking up the mind and escaping from the drowsy
inertia characteristic of human thinking. There are
certain mental qualities we can cultivate that will
awaken ambition, stimulate and clarify the mentality, and subconsciously motivate us so strongly that
we will know ourself to be moving with powerful
tides of enthusiasm and inspiration to accomplish
our goals.

Not only will these right mental qualities act on
the mind to refresh and clarify it, but they are like a
powerful tonic for the physical body as well. Take
hope, for instance. It is usually considered to be a
rather insubstantial tendency in man's makeup
which often deceives him, leads him to cherish illu-
sions and live in expectations that have no solid
foundation in either fact or future possibilities.

But this evaluation of hope is based on incorrect
knowledge of its true nature. It is also based on
man's often disappointing experiences in attaining
his hopes, because he knew neither their source nor
how to sustain hope as a vital factor in accomplish-

ment.

What we ordinarily know as hope is not the genuine thing at all. It is a faint, distorted glimpse of a powerful, vital force inherent in man's mental and emotional makeup. Hope is really one of man's little-known vital forces. The popular saying (which goes back at least to Cicero), "While there's life, there's hope," would be closer to the truth if it were reversed to read, "While there's hope, there's life." Another poet said, "Hope springs eternal in the human breast."

Why not, since hope is one of the essential elements that constitute man's positive vital forces? The quality of hope causes man to expect some boon or benefit. If he only knew how intimately such a hope is part of his own nature, he would be aware that *his hope is caused by the creativeness of life itself,* not by some fancy of his own mind. Hope is not just a mental attribute that causes man to look for the attainment of his desires. Rightly understood, hope is one of the great motive forces of man's soul.* It is not a whim of our mind; it originates at a much deeper level than that, in the very nature of life itself.

A derivative from the original life force that animates man, hope has an inimitable quality in itself; it can confer the essential characteristics of the way a youth feels in the spring upon man's body and mind.

* "You see, hope is a very basic human strength, without which we couldn't stay alive, and not something invented by theologians and philosophers."—*Dialogue with Erik Erikson,* Richard I. Evans; New York, Harper and Row.

It is impossible to describe in words what the deliberate cultivation of hope as a mental or spiritual essence, and its assimilation into the body tissues, can do to man's spirits. All of us have been young. All of us have known the joy of the coming of spring. Can we imagine capturing the very essence of both springtime and youth, and releasing it like a spiritual transfusion into the soul? That is what spiritual meditation on the quality called hope, and spiritual realization of it as an actual impartation to the soul self, can do for both body and mind.

Who would debase his mind and body with so-called mind-expanding drugs (which in reality weaken his will to live and to grow through actual experience, in addition to disorienting his faculty of making right judgments), when he can experience the tingling thrill resulting from genuine, life-imparted hope? This thrill, unlike that gained from drugs, does not lead man to retreat from life by living in fantasies and kaleidoscopic visions which rob him of desire for real accomplishment. No, on the contrary, hope fires man with energy and triggers him to effort in making his hopes come true. It is important that we know this.

Mankind as a whole has entered upon the threshold of a new way of living. We are entering what may be known as the age of soul, of liberation of the psyche, of understanding of man as a soul which is learning to express itself by means of an instrument called a physical body.

Always heretofore, man has thought of himself as a sort of animal possessing higher mental powers than the other beasts. Or if he thought in religious terms, he spoke of "having a soul." What this soul

was, what part it played in life experience, how it
was related to the body . . . these things apparently
were never considered. The soul was deemed to be of
importance only in a "future life," after death had
occurred. No one ever seemed to consider that the
soul, if it did exist, apparently was essential to the
body's being able to sustain life here and now. And
yet, once the precious intangible force called life left
the body, the body was nothing but inert matter. It
was said that the soul had departed from it.

If there is such a thing as the soul, and if it departs
from the body at death, then the soul and the life
force that animates the living body must have a great
deal in common. Someone has said, "Man does not
have a soul, he is a soul." And if man is a soul, then
this soul is a vehicle formed by life itself, for the
purpose of living by means of it. The poet Spenser
knew this. He wrote:

"For of the soul the body form doth take;
     For soul is form, and doth the body make."

If you want your body to retain the desirable
qualities of youth, you should learn by actual experience the power of such a soul force as hope to renew
the body. It is a simple thing to do—that is, if you
know something of meditation, and how to concentrate upon a selected thought. For instance, take this
sentence: "The hope of my spirit is immortal
youth." Concentrate on this by repeating it quietly
to yourself. Think of the quality of hope, of how
closely it seems to be associated with life. Meditate
quietly in this way on hope, and go even further:
affirm prayerfully, "God's Spirit is breathing the
spirit of hope into my soul and body." Do this very
thoughtfully and prayerfully, to end your medita-

tion. Be persistent in doing this every day for two weeks. Then see if your spirits are higher, if you feel more buoyant, more cheerful, if you have more confidence and energy. See whether or not you feel younger. A fair trial will convince you of the incredible power of hope to renew the body. Then you will have no difficulty in believing that man, through the conscious choice of his own mind, expressed in thoughts and words, can actually release a youth-giving tide of soul force into his body, and renew it day by day.

Another vital factor in keeping young is interest. Interest is the polar opposite of boredom. It is a known fact that people can die of sheer boredom. "What is there to live for?" they say. "I've seen this empty show called human life for sixty or seventy years. I'm tired of it." So they begin to withdraw from active participation in life. Perhaps they start to live in the past, and complain that there is nothing new under the sun. This is their conscious or unconscious choice to stop living and start dying. They would be shocked if they were accused of wanting to die, but such an attitude is the "death wish" in action.

However, it could never take over the mind of one who was enthusiastic and interested in some aspect of self-improvement, who had inspired his soul with the secret elixir of youth called hope, and who had some goals toward which he was advancing. I think it was Aldous Huxley who said that there was nothing on the earth as satisfying as the pleasure of advancing, or even at times not advancing, toward some chosen objective.

Do you want to live with the enjoyment of life

that you had when you were young? Remember these important words: *Interest, enthusiasm, hope, and goal-directed activity keep you young.*

How can you stir up more interest in living? There are countless ways. Perhaps you can begin with an affirmation, widely known in the Unity movement: "I am alive, alert, awake, joyous, and enthusiastic about life." If one takes these words into his mind, repeats them silently or audibly as befits the occasion, and tries sincerely to anticipate feeling alive, alert, awake, joyous, and enthusiastic about life, it is impossible not to be infected by the idea these words express. There will be a response on the part of the inner self. It rests with us to accept even a slight feeling of being more alive, and to continue to develop it by more affirmation.

Another way to stir up more interest in life is to concentrate on whatever you are doing in order to do it with your full attention. A tremendous amount of psychic energy leaks away from us because we are not fully absorbed in what we are doing. We do things mechanically, unthinkingly, with our mind far off, the attention not placed anywhere or on anything but occupied in evading the experience of the moment. This weakens the personality and reduces our power to be effective when we really want (or need) to be effective.

One of the great Truth writers of the past century, Prentice Mulford, dwelt much on this theme, that as we increase our power of concentration we increase our energy and strengthen our personality. When we refuse to give our wholehearted attention to whatever we are doing at the moment and give it only a fraction of our attention, we are tacitly trying to escape from life. We are diffusing the power of our mind, wasting the psychic energy which if fully collected and employed would give us the keen enjoyment of experience that children possess.

"Can you tie three knots in a string" asks Mulford, "and give your full undivided attention to tying each one of these knots, and to nothing else, as you perform the act?" Then, "If you can do this, you have permanently increased by a little your power to be alive, to live effectively." No one can force you to make such a simple experiment as this, but you can choose to try it. You can choose to do whatever it is you are doing by entering wholeheartedly into it. You can refuse to do it in your imagination before you actually do it. You can refrain from doing it over and over in your imagination after you do it.

We dissipate startling amounts of psychic energy— first by doing things mentally before we do them, then by refusing to become involved in the actual doing of them, and again by doing them over and over afterward in our imagination, trying to satisfy a secret sense of guilt for not fully giving ourself to the doing of them.

Thus the energy that would give us keen enjoyment of life is frittered away and wasted. Instead of satisfaction, daily life produces vague dissatisfaction, vague anxiety, secret guilt. All this is the result of allowing one's mind to evade its natural mode of employment, which is giving full attention to whatever is being done or thought at the moment.

Why does the mind evade its responsibility in this way? It does not find the matter under consideration interesting, because it has been allowed to indulge in what it finds more pleasant and stimulating (that is, daydreaming and fantasy). However, a strong enough emotion or mood will at once enlist the mind's interest. Enthusiasm is such a dynamic force that the ancients thought it resulted from having a god in oneself.

Can enthusiasm be cultivated by an effort of the will? Can it be simulated at first, until the pretended emotion becomes genuine?

Yes, this can be done. Try it yourself. Take some commonplace task, or better yet, something you have put off doing, and pretend that you are enthusiastically interested in doing it. Imagine yourself plunging into it with the greatest of interest. Affirm that you are enthusiastically and happily doing it. Then begin doing it, and try to sustain the mood. You will be amazed at the results. Enthusiasm can be assumed and acted out; it can be self-generated. Here is another interesting goal-directed activity to help you stay young. Cultivate and develop more and more enthusiasm for being young. Give your enthusiasm a focal point by centering it in this affirmation: *"I am keenly alive and joyously enthusiastic about keeping young."*

Remember that enthusiasm, interest in life, hope, and goal-directed activity keep you young. Have you some clearly defined goals in mind? Do you have target dates for attaining them? What kind of goals are they? Are they involved only with yourself, or are others connected with them? One goal might be to so demonstrate the power of these principles in restoring youth to your body and mind, that you could teach and demonstrate these methods to others. Seeking permanent youth purely for the restoration of sensual enjoyment of life may be self-defeating.

At the very heart and essence of these ideas and principles is the idea that you are first and foremost a mental, spiritual being. You are not an animal that thinks. You do appear to have much in common with the animals. You eat, drink, sleep, assimilate, and eliminate in the same way they do. You even perpetuate your own species in the same way they do. However, it is a grave error to say that you are entitled to act like an animal because you are like them in many respects. You are also unlike the animals in other, very important respects, and it is these unlikenesses that separate you forever from the animal kingdom. They also impose upon you responsibilities far different from those of the animals.

An animal is responsible only for being an animal. It cannot choose to be otherwise, since its intelligence is at all times instinctive and therefore conditioned to act within the limits of its own species.

Considered on the basis of his customary behavior as a species, man also might reasonably be accused of having only an instinctive, preconditioned intelligence which makes his behavior in any important area of life reasonably predictable. It seems that no matter how nobly he may talk of a higher way of life, including peace on earth, he relapses periodically into the stupidity of war and barbarism. So far, this must be admitted as factually evident.

But we make a serious mistake if we stop at what is factually evident when we are seeking to assess the true spiritual possibilities of man. The greater part of what really constitutes man is made up of the tantalizing intangibles that he exhibits. These take the form of aspirations to transcend all his factual performances, and the nobility, self-sacrifice, and heroism he often displays in what may be his worst moments.

How can we disregard the peaks of man's spiritual achievements and accept only the humdrum valleys of his ordinary experience, if we are honestly trying to establish his true potential? To do this is contrary to any scientific procedure. We must take into account all of man's possibilities if we are to make an accurate appraisal of him.

It is not only the long record of semi-animal behavior, but the equally long record of spiritual aspiration and accomplishment that must be taken into account in the history of mankind. Just as a gold-bearing quartz outcrop on the side of a mountain testifies to the rich mine waiting to be developed far below, so do man's continual aspirations, dreams, longings, and idealism testify to the riches of that kingdom that Jesus said was within us all.

The true reason, then, for seeking to cultivate permanent youthfulness in mind and body is to prove the fact that we are not an animal, but a living Spirit. This living Spirit is an ever evolving, growing soul in its relations with the natural world. It needs just such a body as we have in order to become aware of its God-given powers, to test them, try them out, and gain mastery of them through actual experience.

This living Spirit in us, being nonmaterial, is not subject to natural laws or laws of matter. People of most religious faiths believe that this higher or nonmaterial part of us is immortal, that it survives the death of the body. What we are beginning to see now is that if this immortal Spirit is given a body to use and live in, and if this body itself is a divine creation—which it has to be—then why should this body be considered inferior to the soul and Spirit which apparently form it and animate it?

Isn't it possible that we have been making the mistake of trying to understand or evaluate this house of wonders we call a physical body by inadequate means? How can the senses, which are so restricted in their range, and the intellect, which is so inferior in speed, precision, and power, tell us the truth about our body? Could a blind man ever really be an astronomer? Could a deaf man ever enjoy a robin's song in the spring?

One goal each of us might select is to really know ourself, know something of ourself from the inner spiritual standpoint. This is a logical correlative to the discovery of our inner power to stay truly young. Of course we have the goal of cultivating permanent youth.

Not, it is hoped, for the mere physical benefits alone, though they are highly rewarding. Not so we can boast about the number of years we have lived, though this can be pleasing to the ego. But rather for the sake of learning to live from a higher level than the unthinking multitudes who, blindly and unhappily following the footsteps of their grandfathers, walk the way of age and time.

No more pertinent question could be asked than this: When you find the youth of soul and body you are cultivating, what do you plan to do with it? When you find it, you are going to face the fact that it is divine in nature and origin. Let us remember that life knows how to safeguard its essential divinity and protect it from purely selfish exploitation for mere physical gratification.

The nearer you come to the inner Secret, the more softly you should walk. Pray for wisdom. *"Father of my whole being, give me wisdom to use wisely the new life in soul and body as I find it. May I walk the way of life, and help others to discover it. Amen.*

According to the Monterey Herald, Third Mate Leon W. Blachutta has returned to active duty at sea after seven years of retirement. By his example of supervising the loading of supplies for troops abroad he hopes to inspire others, and so relieve the shortage of crewmen. Blachutta is eighty years of age. He looks fit and well.

A number of years ago in Nova Scotia, Silas McLellan, a farmer, ran down strayed cattle on foot. At the age of fifty-six, Silas could run fifty miles as easily as some people walk a mile. He said that he didn't get warmed up in less than twenty-five miles, and was just getting his bearings at forty miles. Sometimes he ran down deer on foot, running from dawn to dusk.

In Amherst, Massachusetts, some years ago, Mrs. Lois Mitchell resumed horseback riding at the age of ninety-four. She rode a horse for the first time in seventy years, and loved it, but complained that the animal didn't have much spirit. "I had to whip him to make him trot," she said. Mrs. Mitchell preferred bicycling to horseback riding, because, as she said, "I can put more vim into it."

# Chapter VIII

*The Building Blocks of Life*

"You Are What You Eat" was the rather sensational title of a book published several years ago. The author of course did not intend that his statement should be taken literally. No one in his right mind would contend that because I eat an egg, I am an egg; or that if I eat a peanut, I am a peanut. What a life of kaleidoscopic changes one would lead if this were true! Since the average male in our country leans heavily to meat and potatoes in his dietary preferences, he would spend much of his time alternating between being roasted, fried, or boiled!

Surely what this author must have had in mind was the fact that the physical body is sustained only by energy. Much of this energy is generated by the body from the digestion, assimilation, and refinement of substances found in various forms of living matter. These substances or food elements are from different sources, and therefore embody differing elements in their composition. Some foods are from the animal kingdom, such as meat, fish, eggs, milk, and cheese. Some are from the vegetable kingdom, such as the cereals, bread, vegetables, nuts, and fruits. A small proportion may be from the mineral kingdom, such as mineral salts in certain foods, and even the water found in living organisms of all kinds.

The undeniable fact is that food does produce energy according to its character. A bowl of bread and warm milk is not calculated to stimulate the one who eats it to physical exertion, but rather to cause sleepiness, induced by comfort and physical gratification. Athletes as a rule prefer thick steaks which stimulate their glands and contribute to explosive energy, in addition to nourishing the tissues.

Anyone who doubts that the nature of the food he eats is directly related to his mental and emotional attitudes could experiment by going on a bland, nonstimulating liquid diet for a few days. He could observe his emotional reactions during this time, and determine whether he was less aggressive, less inclined to irritation and annoyance, than when following his normal diet. He would probably discover that the bland liquid diet tended to make him more placid and even-tempered, less inclined to express annoyance when he felt it.

We are what we eat, to a limited extent. In the most obvious sense, we are more likely to be energetic if we are well and adequately nourished than if we are suffering from famine or pronounced undernourishment. The victims of scurvy in the old sailing-ship days were sick because what they ate did not contain the needed vitamin C. They lacked energy and experienced the other distressing symptoms of this disease because of their diet. When lemon or lime juice was provided, they recovered. They became healthy because of what they ate.

However, in discussing the part that food plays in maintaining youthfulness, we need to stress the fact that *how* we eat is more important than *what* we eat. This refers to our mental attitude while eating. It applies even more to our understanding of the relationship between food and the inner life of the body which accepts the food eaten, assimilates it, apportions it, and finally converts it into the vital energy that sustains our physical body and even our personality.

The influence of the mind on the body is very great; of that we are all aware. But perhaps we have much to learn about the influence of the mind on the body's mysterious assimilative processes, also the various chemical reactions induced in our cell functions not only by substances in foods, but by the direct effect of certain thoughts or emotions.

For instance, scientists have observed that when he was merely reminded of past frustrations or disappointments, strong acid was poured out "by the cupful" into the stomach of a certain man, and the stomach walls became flushed and swelled. Though no food had been taken into the stomach, it reacted just as though it had received something to digest. Does this indicate that a process of digestion also occurs in a symbolic, nonphysical way in man, and that an individual endeavors to "digest" all experiences as they occur, or perhaps that he should digest all significant experiences *after* they occur?

For example, if, as we say, we cannot "stomach" a certain experience, we really mean that we have not been able to react with mastery to it; we do not know how to handle it. Hence it remains buried and "figuratively speaking" undigested, to plague us.

It seems logical to assume that since emotions totally unconnected with the digestion of food, such as the memory of past frustrations, can cause the physical stomach to act as if it had received food, and make it pour out the powerful acids used in beginning the process of digestion, then there must also be a symbolical form of digestion which occurs on the nonphysical level, and reacts on the physical body. That is, anything experienced by the individual in his outward life, any event or occurrence significant enough to cause a marked feeling reaction, is apparently treated as "food" by his nonphysical organism (which we may call the soul).

The soul is really the master mechanism which energizes both mind and body. It contacts the pure life energy of the Creator, and "steps it down," so to speak, transforming it into the mental and physical energy used in daily life.

Man's soul is an infinitely complex and miraculous organism. It is nonphysical in character but is able to manifest and express on the physical or material level, by means of maintaining the flesh body for this purpose. However, the soul, although it permeates the physical organism and energizes it, also maintains an existence of its own on a higher vibrational level than that of the body. The body functions, such as those of digestion, assimilation, and elimination (with which we are so familiar, and which are so vitally necessary to life), are in reality only counterparts of similar faculties that function in identical ways in the soul.

The human body is of course a living organism, but the human soul is even more of a living organism. Apparently, as we have said, it treats earthly experiences as our body treats food. When partaking of physical food we either accept it and digest it, or (if we do not like it or feel it is not good for us) refuse it. In the same way, the soul must accept and digest its earthly experiences, or in some manner reject and refuse them.

The essential thing to understand is that our

experiences in daily life are actual food for the soul. The soul requires this "food of experience" in order to grow, just as the body of a child requires food in order to grow. Our soul must digest these experiences, just as our body digests its food.

When we learn that we can call upon the power of our higher Self to digest the essential lesson of any experience, what a tremendous difference this can make in our life! With sufficient understanding, we can even draw upon spiritual power to reject the psychic consequences of a painful or humiliating experience, and emerge from it unharmed, perhaps even stronger.

Some of these experiences are painful, some are distressing, some are shocking to the soul. What adult person has not experienced the pain of humiliation or failure? Who has not been insulted, or felt at some time rejected or unloved? Who has not smarted under what he felt was injustice, or raged secretly or openly when defeated or frustrated? No one can escape such experiences entirely. They are a part of human life, as it is lived by our species on the level of enlightenment we permit ourselves today.

As a rule we do try to do something about unpleasant experiences. We seek to counteract their effect on our self-esteem in many ways. We attempt to discover reasons for them, or we blame other persons for being the cause of them, or we rationalize about them in a way that comforts our hurt feelings. Sometimes we react constructively by analyzing the occurrence, looking at it calmly, and making mental notes of how we might have avoided it, or what attitude to adopt toward it now.

These are all instinctive attempts to duplicate on

the mental and emotional level the digestive processes that occur on the physical level. They are prompted by the innate wisdom of the soul, and are the best means for digesting experience that the average person knows.

Here is a valuable suggestion: Why not consciously invoke the power of God to help you spiritually digest the emotional reactions to any trying experience? I know this works, because I have done it. On one occasion when I was attending a convention a number of things occurred that aroused deep feelings of grief, anger, and shock among those present. A day or two later my eyes seemed to be inflamed. They watered constantly, burned, itched, and were sensitive to light. I could not relieve the situation by prayer or affirmation, perhaps because I was traveling and had no opportunity to be alone. When at length I could go apart and relax, I received this idea: The power of Spirit digests my emotional reactions to this experience.

At once I began to feel relief. Soon my eyes felt cool and comfortable, and there was no return of the condition. I made a note of the treatment, and passed it on to others when they were reacting emotionally to some unpleasant experience. It is remarkably effective. This treatment could be used in healing any condition rooted in emotional reactions to the actions of others.

We could also take a lesson from our extremely efficient body mechanism, and step up our emotional digestive power to handle experiences. We know that the body, when its vital forces are high, has much greater power to digest food and assimilate it than when it is weak or ill. Can we assume that this principle holds good on the soul level as well? Can we in some way raise the vital forces of the soul and strengthen them, in a manner analogous to the way we use exercise, fresh air, and sleep to step up our body forces? If so, perhaps we will find that just as the healthy body takes hardships, stress, and exposure in its stride, so can the healthy soul take experiences which formerly would have crushed it, or caused humiliation and pain, and successfully assimilate the lessons they are meant to convey, converting the emotional reactions into strength of character.

How can we raise or strengthen the vital force of the soul? Well, we can feed them, nourish them, and exercise them. We can feed them with certain positive ideas and selected emotions. We can nourish them by practice of meditation on spiritual themes. We can exercise them by practicing the expression of wholesome emotions, constructive emotions, in our relationships with other people. In other words, we can stoke up our soul furnace so that it glows with vitally attractive energy, born of such healthful soul foods as love, generosity, joy, good will, forgiveness, and peace. Love of that which is beautiful, good, and true is a potent force in both mental and physical good health. Therefore we must take care to cultivate the growth and increase of love in our emotional nature.

This does not necessarily mean more love in the erotic sense of the word. Rather, it means the cultivation of those qualities associated with the non-erotic expression of love: good will, a determination to treat others kindly, to be patient with their mistakes, or to be forbearing when they offend us. It means the careful nourishing of an even temper, not envying the gifts or good fortune of others, trying to forgive and forget when we have been wronged.

It has never been suggested to us that one of the reasons Jesus urged us to be loving toward our enemies was because of the remarkable results to be expected in developing our soul muscles.

Like all great mystics, Jesus was a supremely practical person. He is usually pictured as concerned only with the salvation of man's soul, in order to save it from "endless punishment" in the next world. However we are now rediscovering that the word *salvation* has a much more practical meaning than its customary theological interpretation.

To quote from the magazine Sharing: "This phrase from Luke 1:77 reading 'knowledge of salvation,' in the Latin reads 'scientia salutis,' which might quite properly be translated 'the science of health' and is so translated in the Wycliffe version of the Bible, though the spelling is Chaucerian."

Dr. John Gayner Banks, in the same article, also says: "Imagine the consternation of the people if a modern Protestant minister announced his text some fine Sunday morning—'Thou shalt go before the face of the Lord, . . . to give the science of health unto his people by the remission of their sins.'

"Every Christian—no matter what his church, or background, or religious affiliation—might profitably bear in mind that the 'knowledge of salvation' and the 'science of health' are interchangeable phrases. Perhaps we will become more zealous in acquiring this sort of 'knowledge of salvation' when we realize that it includes also the elements of health and healing."

No matter how startling it may be to think of the

great word *salvation* having such a practical meaning as this, we must agree that this usage is sanctioned not only by the root meaning of the word itself, but by the constant concern of the Great Physician for the health of people's bodies. He "saved" people from sickness, deformity, blindness, paralysis, even from death. And He was careful to point out that this was a result of His using the power of God to forgive the sins of those who were saved from these physical conditions.

If sin is a condition of the soul, as the Christian church has always maintained, and if this condition of sin in the soul affects the physical body, resulting in sickness, or some physical defect, as Jesus certainly implied in His healing work, then is it not time we conceded that the only real proof of salvation of the soul is the restoration of the body to its original perfection as a work of God? Certainly the perfection of the body would not include age or decrepitude.

As proof of His power to forgive sin, Jesus told the paralyzed man to get up and walk. The man immediately rose, folded up his quilt bed, and walked in a normal manner. The sin in his soul being forgiven, its outward counterpart, called paralysis, was also forgiven. Therefore it vanished from existence in the sight of man, just as it had ceased to exist in the sight of God.

All this is cited to show the highly practical nature of the religious instruction given by Jesus. When He tells us to forgive the offenses of others against us, it is not only for the health of our soul. It is also for the health of our body, for our peace of mind and happiness. And even more, it is for the purpose of developing spiritual robustness of character, moral muscle. We must have this strength of character if we are going to live as Christians in a world which constantly tries to intimidate us by the power of evil, constantly tries to tempt us by the attractiveness of evil, and constantly tries to hypnotize us by the overwhelming weight of appearances that because "everybody" is in bondage to evil, evil must be good.

If we want to cultivate permanent youth, to escape the sentence of old age, decrepitude, and untimely death already passed upon us by the nearly unanimous consent of humanity to ancient superstitions, we will need all the help we can get. It will take moral muscle and strength of character to defy the widespread, unquestioning acceptance of time as the cause of aging. Well-meaning friends will tell us that everybody must get old, wear glasses, become feeble, and finally die from some ailment. Who are we to defy this accepted order of things?

It reminds me a little of Mrs. Henry's starling, Birdee. Mrs. Henry had developed the habit of talking to her pet, so one morning she said to the starling, "Hello, Birdee, what would you like?" The answer came loud and clear: "Bread, please." At first she was unable to believe her ears. As she told her family later, she felt at that moment as though she were a character in a Walt Disney cartoon. Then, trying to be casual, she looked into Birdee's cage. His food bowl was empty. "I guess you're right, Birdee," she said apologetically, and gave him some bird seed. "Thanks," said Birdee.

From that time Birdee kept on talking, until he became famous. Residents of Bowmanville, Ontario, came to the Henry home to hear the "talking bird."

Scientific authorities were consulted, and they declared, "Starlings don't talk." However Birdee defied science and kept on talking. "Busy!" he would screech when one of the family picked up the telephone. And he was usually right, since it was a rural party line.

Birdee consistently identified himself with humans, and not with the animal kingdom. When a farm dog sneaked into the living room for a little nap, Birdee would scold, "Get out of here!" But most amusing of all, when he saw other birds flitting around outside, he felt that this was abnormal behavior and all wrong for birds. "Naughty, naughty!" he would shriek. "Get back in your cage! Get back in your cage!"

What are we going to say when well-meaning but "age-conditioned" people scold us: "Get back in your cage of age! Who do you think you are?" Well, I would like to think that I am a spiritual pioneer, just as my hardy ancestors were political, social, and physical pioneers. The age of the covered wagon, the jolting, arduous journeys across prairies, deserts, and mountains has long since gone. Now we can fly across the land and even across the ocean at a speed so great that we can literally "stay in the sun." Physical science has made this possible.

Should we not expect a spiritual science, if it is truly spiritual and truly scientific, to furnish us with equally startling powers to surmount obstacles in the way of spiritual progress, to transcend time and space in our pursuit of the truth that will make us free from the mind of matter?

*I cannot grow old. God's eternal life force constantly rejuvenates itself in me.*

Should not our spiritual science of today, including the science of health, enable us to draw on the best of the spiritual illuminations of the past, even those that have been forgotten, or lost to us by the passage of time? Should it not also anticipate the discoveries certain to be made in the future in the realm of mind and Spirit? And should not these discoveries emancipate us from much that we now believe to be binding in these matters of longevity and health? I think it only reasonable to expect that it should.

These are all highly relevant ideas in connection with the idea of nourishing the soul, in order that it may sustain its physical counterpart in continuing youth and strength. You can feed and exercise and strengthen your soul, you can warm it with love and exercise it with discipline of the feeling reactions, just as surely as you now feed, exercise, and strengthen your body.

We need to understand that this physical body, which human opinion has been taught to consider highly perishable, is made of the same substance as the most durable and long-lived materials known on earth. Science now tells us that the only real difference between one form of material substance and another is in the way the atoms dance around each other. The difference between a diamond and a lump of clay is not that they are of different material, but that the atoms composing both are the same, but dancing to different tunes.

To quote John J. Grebe, nuclear scientist: "It is now recognized that the very tune sung by each electron whirling around the nucleus of its hydrogen atom when the atom is living differs by precisely

measured rates from the same structure of the atom
when it is dead. This is measured by new instruments
which grip the molecule in a magnetic vise and then
twang it as though it were a reed, to amplify its
natural oscillation. It is called electron spin reso-
nance."

Can we possibly learn to make the atoms of our
flesh dance to a different tune than that of inevitable
decay and old age? Spiritual intuition and the logic
of mind insist that we can. We have been entrusted,
you and I, with some precious gifts from the great
creative Force that made us and set us to evolving. A
little more knowledge of these gifts, holding in their
possession miraculous possibilities far beyond fairy
tales, will enable us to perform miracles in the field
of mind and spirit, just as our brothers in the fields of
physics and mechanics have opened new worlds and
hurled us forward by light years, through their discoveries in the world of matter.

It is a little saddening to read some of the metaphysical books of the previous century. What miracles they expected the new spiritual knowledge of
the laws of mind to accomplish! In the 1890s the
writers were expecting the world to be transformed
into the kingdom of heaven in half a century. How
shocked they would have been had they been able to
see the world racked by the greatest war of all time in
just fifty years! Could they have believed that today,
nearly a hundred years after the beginning of mental
healing on this continent, their wonderful new
"science" of healing and transformation through
mind would still be struggling for a foothold, still be
snubbed and denied by most of the professions?

No doubt today we are ready to proclaim that at

last Truth is knocking at the door of our solidly entrenched human beliefs. So it is, but is anybody at home? We must all be a great deal more daring, a great deal more persistent, a great deal more hardy in standing up to conventional human belief, if we are ever to have that golden age our spiritual forefathers predicted.

We must be brave enough, like Ali Baba, to speak the magic words and enter the doors of the treasure cave, which are now partially open to our unbelieving gaze. What are the treasures we see? Gifts of the gods that we have been using without thought and without esteem, such as the mysterious thing called metabolism.

Webster's Collegiate Dictionary defines metabolism, in part, as "the chemical changes in living cells, by which the energy is provided for the vital processes and activities, and new material is assimilated to repair the waste."

These chemical changes by which the cells of the body renew themselves are so complicated that it would be impossible (and inadvisable) for me to attempt any description of them. A physicist has said that the renewal of the body cells would have its parallel in a house if old bricks were constantly being removed and new bricks put in. What is even more wonderful, the "body house" manufactures in itself the bricks or building blocks of which it is composed!

If we had a house which constantly repaired and restored and repainted itself, and replaced any worn-out or decayed material in itself, by itself, that house would be the talk of the world. Scientists would come from all nations to observe it, test it, and seek to understand the processes by which it did these miraculous things.

Of course you and I know that we live in such a house right now. In the time it has taken you to read these lines, your body house has taken out and replaced millions of these "bricks" called cells. The great majority of the body cells—the entire molecular cellular structure—is turned over, and replaced at regular intervals, in some cases in an extremely short time. Surely we should be willing to learn more about this wondrous house of the soul which we know as our physical body, since its marvels surpass the mind of man. One of its greatest wonders is the magnificent maintenance service called metabolism.

It is said that in youth, the rate of metabolism is high. In age, it is said to slow down. In other words, a youthful body quickly digests and assimilates required nourishment, and carries on this process of cell replacement at high speed. Thus a youthful person normally has great recuperative power. Energy is restored quickly through food and rest. Resistance to stress in the form of illness is high. Children lost in the wilds sometimes endure exposure, cold, and hunger without harm, because of their superior vitality and reserve forces. Their body heat is a continual surprise to adults. All this is connected with a high rate of metabolism.

In seeking to regain and enjoy what the British Nobel Prize winner Sir George Thomson has called "permanent youth," we should prayerfully consider whether metabolism with all its marvels is a purely physical process, or whether it derives its being and powers from the intangible but very real part of us called the soul.

If the metabolism of the body is animated and empowered by the soul, then we should be able, through our deeper inner mental processes, to stimulate and restore this metabolism, when it seems to have slowed down or have less recuperative powers.

These building blocks of life called cells, which in turn are created and recreated constantly by the metabolism of the body, need actual physical substances in the form of food and drink to construct themselves. This nourishing material is first taken into the mouth, and (in the case of solid food) reduced to a liquid before being swallowed. There is a teaching that man can impress on any food or drink taken into his mouth, while he is chewing it, certain thoughts that will greatly enhance the energy-producing qualities of the food. In fact, he can, if he chooses, decide at the moment of mastication that this food shall yield increased strength, that it shall be completely satisfying to his appetite—and this thought, impressed upon his food, will in time cause him to have increased energy as well as satisfaction.

The practice of blessing food before eating it is no doubt based upon this principle. Can we experiment with this idea in our cultivation of youthful energies? Yes, but it must be done with discretion. Man never knows what fantastic powers he has at his disposal, and what drastic effects the unwise use of these powers can produce in his body, until he experiments with something like this. Use this great principle of "thought chewing" while physically chewing, with a deep desire to be guided by wisdom in its right use. The results will probably astound you.

What you are really using is a form of mental metabolism. By this "thought chewing" you are impressing on the nonmaterial energies contained in the cells of the food a different rate of vibratory action than they would have in their natural state. Consequently when they are reduced to their final form for absorption by the cells, they will embody a higher vibratory energy than that to which the cells are accustomed.

The effect of this can be very upsetting to the cells unless great moderation is used. Start with "thought chewing" just one mouthful of food at a meal. Gradually increase this to two mouthfuls, then three, then to any proportion of the food taken at one meal. As soon as you experience a feeling of increased energy and well-being, you may increase the extent to which you practice "thought chewing" . . . but still with discretion.

What thought should you impress upon your food? If you customarily bless your food, start with: *God blesses and adapts this food to the renewing of my body.* For those who like affirmations, *God substance in this food is strength for me* would be excellent. If you are not used to the idea of blessing your food, think: *I chew this food carefully to produce extra strength.*

Different qualities may be selected, such as: I chew this food carefully to produce satisfaction. But here again, much depends on how you do this simple exercise. If you put your thought into it, "mix" the selected thought with the food, so to speak, at the moment you eat it, you will, if you persist, obtain striking results. But if you think this idea is too strange, or that it is too much like "occultism," or that it is too simple to bother with, naturally you will get no results.

If you want to have the light and buoyant step of youth, if you want to walk as if your feet were cushioned on springs, if you want to restore the gusto for life you had as a youth, to plunge happily into each day just because you are glad to be alive, then you should try this "mental metabolism" method for building up youthful energy.

To be young, yet mature: that is the unspoken desire back of all the fables about the fountain of youth, isn't it? Many of us can testify that the time of our physical youth was not all pure happiness. We faced so many new experiences, so many unknown quantities, that the years of youth sometimes brought unhappiness and sufferings. Now with our greater experience, we can enjoy our new mature youthfulness more than we ever enjoyed adolescence or the various stages of physical youthfulness.

The word *maturity* has a different meaning in this context of permanent youth than it had before. For those who are very young, maturity means being old. For the one cultivating permanent youth, maturity implies peak performance in expressing youthfulness. Originally the word *mature* carried the meaning of being ripe, ready for harvest. We keep this meaning in the sense of seeing our youthfulness always maintained at a peak of enjoyment, energy overflowingly ready for use.

Remember too the well-loved saying: "No one ever grows old. He gets old because he stops growing." This is true. If you want to live, you must grow. Life will not let you stand still. Grow you must. Why "grow old" when you can grow young? This is a simple choice, but one that cannot be escaped. Either grow or give up. To stay youthful, you should grow in experience, grow in knowledge, grow in livingness. Above all, you should grow in deeper understanding of your identity with life itself.

Gaylord Hauser says, "Mental stimulation is the only way currently known by which our nerve cells can ward off death for themselves." The constant stimulation of the brain cells by new ideas is a vital necessity if we are to surmount the various forms of belief in age. Keep up those exercises in mind renewal described in Chapter IV.

Remember that it is not Nature that makes us old! If we understood properly our relationship to Nature, it would be impossible for us to grow old. Nature is simply overflowing with vivifying, rejuvenating agencies, a vast, infinite storehouse of vital energy, immortal in essence, immanent in its presence, nonmaterial in its character. Our mind was created to understand, lay hold of, and turn these forces into channels of healing and renewal. We believe that Jesus used them constantly. With a prayer for wisdom, you and I can do likewise.

In 1961 Jesse Cox, age 92, applied for a marriage license in Los Angeles. Mr. Cox, a Cherokee Indian, was a scout with the Seventh Cavalry in 1895-1896. He traveled with Buffalo Bill and Annie Oakley as a rider in their show, and appeared before Queen Victoria in 1901. His bride-to-be was fifty-five. A reporter asked if he planned to carry her over the threshold. "You bet I do, son," Cox replied, picking up his bride-to-be and carrying her into the license bureau. "I'm still a pretty good man!"

In Bartow, Florida, Charlie Smith celebrated his 125th birthday. Charlie, who believes he is the world's oldest man, has a little candy store. He is always happy to spin a few yarns of the days when he was a cowboy and rode the range. He does not know the day he was born, but Social Security officials who checked out his stories are satisfied that his age is as claimed. At the age of 113, Charlie was still climbing ladders as a citrus picker.

# Chapter IX

*Permanent Youth, the Gift of God*

Now we come to the last and, by all odds, the most important of the ideas and the practices by which we are to attain the new-age quality which I have called "permanent youth." It was a British scientist who spoke of youth in terms of being permanent. And if we are honest, most of us will admit that this is what we want. As someone has said, everyone wants to live long, but no one wants to get old. Why should he?

Only God knows the bitterness that is in the hearts of God's children when they first experience the shock of being "old," or the still deeper frustration that seethes within them at being consigned to idleness, uselessness, and inevitable extinction, when all the time something within them protests that they are not old at all. They still feel as young as they ever did, in one part of their being. But the tyrant of "appearances" has judged them and sentenced them.

Old they are by the records of the calendars and the timepieces, old they are by the witness of their children and the endless circling of the earth in its sun-swept path. Old they are sometimes by the witness of feeble bodies, faltering footsteps, and failing memories. So the world of appearances pronounces sentence: "You shall be bound by the word *old* until you are dead. You must retire. We have no use, no place for you. We are too busy."

But you can appeal from this verdict!

Thank God there is a higher court, a higher authority than this tyrant of our human race belief in time and age! The child of God who stands accused or convicted of age does not need to cringe or cower, or stand helpless or alone. He has a champion, an invincible, indomitable counselor who knows how to appeal from this court of the world and its false beliefs to a just Judge and a true world.

In Old Testament times, in the long-forgotten years when the Book of Job was written, the unknown genius who wrote this giant essay of feeble man daring to challenge the great and terrible being called God knew something of this longing to defy age. In the thirty-third chapter of Job, Elihu draws a vivid picture of age and illness. He says:

"His soul draws near the Pit,
and his life to those who bring death.
If there be for him an angel,
a mediator, one of the thousand,
to declare to man what is right for him;
and he is gracious to him, and says,
'Deliver him from going down into the Pit,
I have found a ransom;
let his flesh become fresh with youth;
let him return to the days of his youthful
vigor.'"

Is this just Oriental exaggeration, the typical extravagant language of hyperbole and fairy tale? Who is the "angel," the "mediator," who shows the sick man what is right for him, so that God is gracious to man, and remits the sentence of death? It is said that when this happens, his flesh shall "become fresh with youth;" he shall "return to the days of his youthful vigor."

In modern times when the practice of healing through mental and spiritual agencies is becoming more and more common, the idea of a human being who is seriously ill being restored to health by divine intervention does not seem as incredible to us as it did to our ancestors.

There are many today who will testify that when they were sick, not with imaginary ailments but with ailments that were medically diagnosed, they appealed from the verdict of "incurable," either through their own prayers to a Supreme Being, or through the greater faith and understanding of another person . . . and their well-authenticated ailments disappeared. There are no medical explanations for sure cures. This could be called divine intervention, or the operation of a higher law than the laws of matter or of medicine.

The word *intervention* is not much used in contemporary metaphysical schools, as it suggests a somewhat capricious Higher Power who interferes arbitrarily in human life, and confers benefits or favors on some but not on others. This idea is repugnant to those who believe that God is governed by unfailing law and principle when dealing with man.

Yet there is no violation of law in divine intervention. There is only the perception (either by the sick person or by another) that there is a higher field of forces operating in and through man than the forces of matter. This higher field of forces could be called the "Father" of physical man, which is what Jesus called it.

He said of His healing miracles that they were not His work, but the work of the Father. Let us for a moment take the attitude that all of the physical life of man stems from a higher field of forces, intangible to the senses, called the psychic body, or "soul." Let us further say that this psychic body, called soul, stems from the stepping-down of a still higher and more ethereal level of forces called the Spirit of God. And let us say that the field of forces called Spirit is really the cause of the soul and body being able to function and express as they do. Is it not reasonable to call this power, which begets the existence of the soul and body instant by instant, our "heavenly Father"?

If it is true that the life force which animates and operates our so-called flesh body is nonmaterial in character and constantly originates in a field of forces superior to matter, then we have a reasonable explanation of the miraculous healings performed by Jesus. Suppose that the Master knew and understood that the body and its imperfections were only the surface manifestation of a greatly superior life force, and that this superior life force (which created the body in the first place) had power to re-create it at any time. Then it would be necessary only to appeal to this life force to re-create the ailing part.

Jesus knew how to do this. Apparently He required some form of mental assent by the one being healed. He called this "faith." Often He merely said to the sick person, "Your faith has made you well." Did Jesus have the faculty of quickening this faith in the mind of one who appealed to Him? Was the dynamism inherent in His character and outer appearance such that it kindled an instant belief in His power when people saw Him? Or did He have such tremendous spiritual insight and perception that He could see beyond the mask of human appearance, and clearly behold the soul power potential in the individual's desire? Was it really this ardent longing of the soul to make contact with its spiritual Father and be healed that He called faith? Have we had a wrong definition of faith?

The writer of Hebrews said, "Faith is the assurance of things hoped for, the conviction of things not seen." Is not faith the energy of one's own power to desire, coupled with an intuitive conviction that this desire can be attained? From this standpoint faith is the ardent longing of the soul to have its desire satisfied, and this desire in turn is born of an intuition that the longed-for good can be obtained. Then faith is not a mysterious quality of believing, but *a purpose we believe in.* If we did not intuitively believe in our power to attain this desire, we would not try to get it.

Suppose we were to interpret the Master's often repeated words to sufferers whom He restored, "Your faith has made you well," in this way: "Your longing to be made well is the power that has made you well." Then what part did Jesus play? Countless people before and since have longed to be made well, but this longing did not result in their healing. What did Jesus do that made the difference?

Was He not simply the Angel, the Mediator who "intervened" or interceded for the sick one? To intervene, says Webster, is "to come between as an influencing force." And to mediate is to act through an intervening agency. A mediator is a middleman, one who comes between others to bring about some result.

Could we say, then, that Jesus, when healing the sick or crippled, acted as interpreter of the intense longing in their hearts to be well? Did He not, in a silent flash of soul communion, interpret the sufferer's desire to him as being the very power of God in action, with "healing in its wings"? And in revealing God to the soul of the sick one as being already present, vitally present, in his own desire, the gap was closed. The spark flashed from mind in action as longing, to mind in action as fulfillment of its own longing. There really never was any gap between desire and its fulfillment. They were always the same thing, perceived in two different ways.

The longing, the desire for healing was the power and presence and willingness of life to heal, being only partially perceived through the mind of the senses. The translation of this longing, as communicated in a flash of soul empathy by Jesus, was a superior perception that the desire for wholeness was the wholeness itself, asking, seeking, knocking at the door of the human "I" for acceptance. Being instantly accepted by the soul (and in fact by the whole personality), this conception of wholeness was instantly perceived as healing. "Your longing to be made well is the power that has made you well." Or as it is stated in Biblical language, "Your faith has made you well."

What has this to do with the aged? Their longing to be freed from age is acute. They need an interpreter to show them that their longing is the power that longs to free them from age, and is able and willing to do so. To repeat: the child of God who stands accused or convicted of age does not need to cringe or cower, or stand helpless or alone. He has a champion, an invincible, indomitable counselor who knows how to appeal from this court of the world's false beliefs to a just Judge and a true world.

This counselor is man's own Spirit, his own higher Self, the immortal, eternal undying life within him. What he wants really is to appeal from the world of the flesh to the inner world of the spectacularly intelligent and powerful spiritual mind that animates his own inner world and body cells. But how does one do this?

There is a way, a definite, practical way that can be understood and practiced by everybody. It is a way with which we are already familiar, because we have been using it all our life. It is the way of rest. All of our life we have had to give our body rest in sleep. We inherited this necessity for rest when we were given a physical body through birth, and the need for rest was automatically supplied by certain processes, even yet but little understood. These cause us periodically to be overcome by a need for sleep. During sleep our body is rested and refreshed. Our conscious mind is almost completely blocked out, for from five to eight hours, while this renewal and restoration of the body is carried out. But we do not experience any lessening of our mental faculties through this lapse of consciousness. On the contrary, our faculties function better after it. Our mind is as a rule keener and better able to do anything we ask of it after a good night's sleep than at any other time.

If rest is good for the body and good for the mind, the question naturally arises, is it possible to use this method of renewal in still other ways? Could it be used to rest the nonphysical body of man, usually called the soul? Some may object that the soul being nonmaterial does not need rest, in the way the body does. But if the body derives its primary energy from the soul, does not the soul in turn derive its primary energy from the Spirit? This seems logical. The soul needs to rest by turning itself over to Spirit, just as the body rests by turning itself over to the soul.

The truth is that what we call rest is only a means of restoring rhythm to whatever we are resting. The rest gained by pausing from physical or mental exertion, when we are temporarily fatigued, permits the over-active glands and organs to slow down, to become more rhythmic, more regular in their action. Since the new physics speaks of matter as being essentially musical, and since rest is an essential part of any rhythm or music, then matter is fundamentally action and rest, in a musically ordered interrelation.

But where does this "music" of matter originate? The Book of Job speaks of the morning stars singing together and all the sons of God shouting for joy, at the moment when the cornerstone of the world was laid. Sometimes we read of the harmony of the spheres. The "music" of matter originates in the joy of heaven. Rest of any kind is getting back into the rhythm, into the harmony of that heavenly Presence that pervades all form.

The outer form of rest is what we know as sleep. What is the true meaning of sleep? It is an escape from disorder and confusion, from the welter of conflicting reports given by our senses, from the cares and burdens, the successes or failures of the day. During sleep the inner life, the higher Intelligence which runs the unseen world of the cells, takes over to a certain extent. The vital energies which were all projected and pointed outward during the day flow back into a state of balance once more. The soul, freed from the incessant demands of the senses and their sensations, can and does refresh the body and restore its energies. Is this all that happens during sleep?

By no means. It seems likely that the soul has a holiday of its own while the body is inactive. What really happens in the halls of sleep is a deep mystery (probably a wise provision of nature to prevent us from interfering in it). Some say that the soul during sleep dreams the experiences it is to have during the next day. Others believe that, on the contrary, the soul tries to digest and assimilate during sleep the experiences of the day just ended. Some believe that the soul, free of material restraints, leads an independent existence with other souls, on a nonmaterial level, during sleep.

Some hold that the soul retreats during sleep to the deepest inner levels of its own consciousness and here works out its own destiny. It is felt that the soul renews its contact with the divine Life-Presence during the time when the conscious mind and body are at rest. Who knows what happens during sleep? All that we know for sure is that this period of detachment and rest called sleep is essential for physical and mental well-being.

After a good night's sleep the energy and strength of the body are restored. There is a sense of well-being, a willingness to work. The mind is fresh and functions at its best. The nerves feel steady and strong. The individual feels as though he is a different person than the one who retired to sleep the night before. And indeed he is, in a number of ways.

Chemically speaking, many of the finer elements that constitute the essence of the ductless glands have been changed during the night's rest. The soul can and does manufacture chemicals of its own right in the body. These are so refined, so ethereal in nature, that they have escaped the notice of those who analyze the composition of the human body. Nevertheless we believe they do exist. Just as the existence of vitamins was not scientifically proved until this century, although they had always been a part of living substances, so the existence of these delicate soul chemicals will someday be proved by scientific methods.

Until then let us just accept on faith the idea that rest gained through sleep is absolutely essential to the body and the mind, and its chief benefits are the renewal or restoration of energy to the nervous tissue and brain. Now if such a marked physical renewal can be obtained through the rest that sleep gives, is it possible that a renewal of the soul's energies can be experienced through some form of rest obtained by the soul? And if so, what would be the benefits of such rest by the soul?

The soul, which is a living organism composed of essences and highly refined substances at present not known to man, has its own laws, just as the body has its laws. The soul has periodic inflows of energy which it expends in various forms of activity just as the body does, with this difference: The soul not only requires energy for its own functions, but it must furnish the very considerable quantities of energy required by the body. Apart from the soul, the body has no energy of its own. It is completely dependent on the soul.

Now the soul must receive its inflows of energy from the Life-Presence that animates man. From its point of contact at the crown of the head, the spiritual magnetic life essence is radiated into the soul. It then activates the primary ideas by which the body is empowered. These in turn animate the various functions of the body, and keep them energized so man can live.

If the individual drives and pushes his physical body and attempts to ignore its needs for sleep and rest, this taxes the energies of the soul. It does not have a proper opportunity to do its work for the body. The body suffers. The soul can be overtaxed and actually be fatigued. The individual's whole tone then is lowered—and this is not just a figure of speech. Remember, all matter is essentially musical in nature. It must accord with or be attuned to certain key notes in order to maintain its properties. So when we say that the body tone is lowered, speaking in human terms, we mean that it is not normally healthy or sound.

But speaking in soul terms, we mean that the tone of the organism is actually lowered, that it is not on pitch, not on key; it is not vibrating in tune with its proper musical key of life or strength or love, or other elements in the great harmony of life. So the body suffers. The soul must make greater efforts to keep it energized.

The soul, in this case, does not have time to look after its own needs. It can become fatigued. The individual is weary. He may become bad-tempered or inefficient. This is quite a common occurrence. Sometimes illness causes the individual to take rest. Sometimes spiritual counsel shows him the folly of forcing and driving his body, and he voluntarily changes his ways.

At any rate, be assured that your soul needs rest, just as your body does. The soul is a natural organism and is fed by nature's forces, just as the body is, but the forces on which the soul feeds are finer and higher in vibration, more volatile than those we know as physical substance. There are different ways to rest the soul. For instance, the soul requires beauty just as the body requires food. Beauty in any form is a kind of nourishment for man's soul.

What refreshment man gains from a short walk in the country, or a period of work in his garden! This is because the beauty of nature actually feeds his soul. Works of art also feed the soul. Music is of extreme importance to the soul. The soul also derives much tonic and stimulation from color. Joy of any kind is to the soul as water is to the body. Was it not Emerson who said, "The soul's highest duty is to be of good cheer"? The soul thirsts for joy; it is a necessity.

Those who resort to alcohol, trying to find joy through the toxic stimulation and burning of their finer brain tissues, are victims of a legitimate need for joy, which they are trying to satisfy in an unnatural, debased way. They can be redeemed through learning to think, breathe, eat, and pray in ways that produce joy.

As we said before, true rest is an advanced degree or spiritualized expression of the physical rest that keeps life in this body of ours. In one sense it is a natural process. Man has practiced it for ages—but not under the name of rest. It has been called contemplation, silence, prayer, *satori, samadhi,* meditation, deep meditation, communion, and many other names. But essentially it is a conscious resting or stilling of the human mentality, a quieting of the body and the nerves, a turning inward and upward of the eye of the mind, with the purpose of consciously coming into a perfect balance deep within oneself.

There is a point at which conscious mental activity voluntarily suspends itself, where the presence of a greater Self is sensed, where the body is relaxed and still, and the mind, though it is inactive, is not a blank nor a void. It is just resting, as one might rest at ease on a perfect summer day, with senses all alert, but not thinking—merely enjoying, welcoming, perceiving. This is true rest.

How can one voluntarily put his mind and body into the condition that makes spiritual rest possible? Certain guides can be given: a definite time in which to practice being relaxed in mind and body; a comfortable position, usually seated, both feet flat on the floor, hands open and relaxed, back straight (sit tall!).

Begin with the physical body; seek to quiet and relax the body, bring it to a state of complete stillness. Stop all the twitchings, the involuntary movements; shift the weight until the body is absolutely comfortable and can be still. It often helps to tell the various parts, particularly the eyes, to relax into peace, or strength, or life. Also, get the hands relaxed. The hands and the will act and react on each other: tense will, tense hands; tense hands, tense will.

After bringing the body to a state of relaxed stillness, there is usually little more to do. The conscious intellectual activity has been slowed down. The attention now must be diverted from thinking or holding thoughts or concentrating in any way, to the idea of "watching" or observing oneself in a detached way. There is to be no attempt to get outside of oneself in doing this. Rather the idea is simply to direct the attention to a point of balance, somewhere down behind the physical heart. There one rests in complete abandonment to the sense of "just being." When properly done (and it never can be forced), the results are magical. More can be accomplished in one instant of such spiritual rest than in nights of prayer, or weeks of mental working.

The point is that spiritual rest renews and refreshes the soul, brings it back into harmony with the rhythms of nature. When the soul is renewed it cannot help renewing the body, for the body is really soul perceived through the limitations of the senses. And soul is of course Spirit, or the I AM, perceived through the limitations of the psychic nature. There is only one unlimited perfect Mind and perfect Body, which we perceive "in a mirror, darkly."

Seeing our body through the misty limitations of the senses, we call it young at a certain time of life, middle-aged at a later period, and old a few years later. But this is all a matter of matter, so to speak, and matter means limitation. Limitation is the most characteristic quality of matter. It is this quality of limitation that makes matter so useful to us, and also makes matter harmful to us.

For instance, for a rose to be a rose, the substance caught and fixed in its vibrational patterns (which give it the beautiful form and fragrance of a rose) must be restricted to that form. It cannot be a rose and at the same time be a dahlia or a begonia.

An orange is always an orange. It is limited to being an orange—limited in size and form and color and composition. That is what makes it an orange, not an apple or a peach. Anything material is always limited. When we believe our body to be material it must be limited in its appearance to us. Because we do believe our body to be material, we have fixed an entirely artificial limitation on the length of time the body can function efficiently. Usually based on a misunderstanding of the 90th Psalm, we fix this period at seventy to eighty years. But there are so many people now ignoring this threescore-and-ten syndrome, and living in the best of health far beyond it, that its absurdity is becoming recognized. Soon its binding power on human life expectancy will be considered a ridiculous superstition. It will be discarded, just as the notion that night air was harmful, which made our forefathers sleep with their windows closed, was discarded. Many who read this will remember encountering this belief at an early age; today we believe that the more fresh air we can get during sleep, the better. So we open our windows and let the air in, night or day.

It is high time we opened the windows of our mind to the fresh air of new ideas. As Ella Wheeler Wilcox said: "Tear away the blinds of superstition, let the light pour through fair windows, broad as Truth itself, and high as heaven." The belief that we have a material body, limited by the laws of matter and the laws of nature to a certain number of years on the earth, will not stand the test of logic. Both the Old and the New Testament firmly proclaim that God is omnipresent. In our body is part of the omnipresence of God.

If God is truly omnipresent, as the Bible says, why should that omnipresence stop and cease to be, wherever the body begins? "But we have a material body." If the presence of God fills heaven and earth, can anything exist apart from it? Can even so-called matter exist apart from the presence of God?

The attempt to separate the presence of God from the presence of matter is as fruitless as the attempt to draw a dividing line between body and mind. Who can say: "Here mind ends. Here body begins."? If the body has any reality at all, is it not mind orga- nized and functioning in substance, mind perceived through the limitations of the physical senses?

It is time we reacted to the saying, "There is no matter, all is mind," not by attempting to separate something that seems to be material from something called mind, but by including whatever seems to be material in the realm of mind. A slang saying was, "Include me out." We have been including the body out of Spirit and mind. Now we must "include it in."

Thirty years ago I had my first illumination on this subject, and wrote an article about it which was published in Science of Mind magazine under the title "This Way to Heaven." I remember the reaction of a practitioner of spiritual healing, a close family friend, when I sent her some ideas along this line many years ago. She reacted with what was almost a holy horror: "What are you trying to do, Russell, make matter real?" She could not have been more shocked if I had asked her to invite the Devil to lunch. To her, schooled as she had been for years in the uncompromising denial of matter, in the implicit belief that all the ills and troubles of humanity have their origin in the "belief" in matter, this was an attack on all she held dear and lived by. She had no choice but to reject it.

Yet she also had no choice but to use matter, even in rejecting my theories. When she wanted to convey to me by letter her abhorrence of my approach to the problem of matter, she used such material substances as paper, pen and ink, and a postage stamp. Every breath she drew (eighteen or twenty of them a minute) was of a material substance called air. A material train carried her letter to me. But of what use to argue? I could have pointed out that Emma Curtis Hopkins, after spending most of her life in the "absolute" approach to metaphysics, said, "The endurance and substantiality of matter have been far better proved than its opposite." But Mrs. Hopkins had been cast out of the movement many years before, and therefore belonged to those metaphysical untouchables whose heretical ideas were anathema to the leader. "No, no, matter is unreal!" Well, unreal or not, the metaphysicians of the last century, in spite of all their brave denials, in the end surrendered to matter as tamely and obediently as did the earthworms beneath their feet. Loudly proclaiming "There is no matter," they met their end either from sheer weight of years and decrepitude or from other "material" causes.

So we see that the denial of matter will not deliver us from its limitations. It is, in my opinion, only the spiritual understanding of matter that will deliver us from its so-called laws and power.

In fact, I do not believe that there is any one thing alone that will enable us to overcome the material race belief in age and time. I do not think that any amount of brave "treatments," no matter how beautifully they are worded, will do it. Make all the treatments you please. If you depend on them alone,

shirk exercise and physical activity, scorn the role
played by proper nutrition, and drive your body
unmercifully, someday you may find yourself
saying: "I'm getting a little older, a little fatter! Is
this funny little guy who is getting older really me?
What has happened to me? And there's nothing I can
do about it!"

But there is! Wake up to the fact that you can't do
it all with your mind. Stop fighting your greatest
servant, matter, and learn to use it. Pray for and
appropriate wisdom. Wisdom will enable you to
understand nature. Nature is not your enemy; nature
is your friend, your arcane storehouse of life, and
your treasure cave of wealth. Nature is only a name
for the "Mother" side of God. If we understood only
a little of what nature holds in store for us, if we
could accept even a little of the energy the golden
sun beams upon us every day, it would be impossible
to grow old.

"Tear away the blinds of superstition." Can there
be metaphysical superstitions already when our
Truth movement is barely a century old? Think for
yourself; experiment for yourself. Reject, if need be,
everything you have been told about metaphysics.
Affirm faithfully that the unfaltering light of God in
your own soul reveals to you the truth about the
nature of the world in which you live. Then you will
be ready for your own new age, which is "no age,"
but permanent youth.

Your desire for youth and rejuvenation is God's
desire for you to have them. React to this desire in a
positive way. What you are experiencing as desire is
actually the divine, indomitable urge of the true life
force within you to live and fulfill its nature through

you.

You must disregard all the conventional ideas of age, all the accepted material or religious ideas about the inevitability of age. The only thing you need to know about age is that you are now living in the first days of the "new age." This is a "new age" book. The ideas in it are new. Its approach to the great central problem of matter is new. Its message—that time of itself has no power to cause age—is also new.

Don't let yourself be frightened by these ideas. Keep on reading and thinking about them. Soon they will seem quite reasonable. They *are* reasonable from the standpoint of the new physics which is being evolved now. In a few years the present form of belief in the reality of matter will be out of date. YOu do not need to wait for that time. Join the human race of tomorrow, today!

What will the human race of tomorrow be like? It will probably be in various stages of civilization and advancement, just as it is today. But what will the truly enlightened man of tomorrow be like? He will be a great deal more like the man God "invented" than he is today. The man God envisioned and ideated was of course an ideal man, a perfect man. This does not mean a static, unchanging perfection. Cora Dedrick Fillmore, in her book *Christ Enthroned in Man,* said of Jesus' saying "You, therefore, must be perfect": "The original meaning of that word *perfection* is the strength to carry to completion an idea or a plan formed in the mind."

So the perfect man of tomorrow will be one who is sufficiently awakened from the sleepy material race belief to be aware of his divine potential and resources, aware that he is equipped with the strength to make his spiritually inspired dreams come true, aware of the will and determination to persist until he actualizes them in his own flesh.

Can you believe that God's man, the man of tomorrow, is what you are today? You can become aware of it as you read, assimilate, and practice the ideas in this book. They will gradually change your whole way of thinking about so-called age. Gradually you will so incorporate these ideas into your own philosophy that age reckoned by your birth certificate will be just a statistic to you. It will be a useful statistic for a long time to come, but it will no longer have the power to tell you when you are to stop living and enjoying life.

Just think what all of us have been doing: giving to our birth date the power to cause our demise! Does this seem reasonable? Should a birth date, a mere point in time, have more power than God? Think about this.

Remember the saying, "It isn't what you used to be, it's what you are today"? It is still valid, so let's accept it. We used to be people who believed in the power of time to make us old. But now we are not what we used to be, for we have exposed the fallacy of this "time neurosis." Forward-thinking medical science has urged us to reject it. Biologists, zoologists, researchers in many branches of science have shown us the wonders of our body dwelling, and its power to renew and restore itself.

We used to be people under a sentence of untimely death, based on mistaken beliefs in the cumulative power of years to produce age. Today we are, I hope, people who dare to think of ourselves in a new way, as God's new people, the people of tomorrow.

And it's what we are today that counts.

Today there are increasing numbers of hardy, inspired persons everywhere (and God bless them!) who are already defying the accepted, conventional beliefs in old age and living happy, active lives, regardless of their years. I once heard one of these men, over eighty but still active and vigorous, interviewed on a radio program. To the inevitable question, 'How old are you?" he replied: "God gives us life, not age. I am alive. Thank God!"

Let us stop arguing humanly; let us learn to argue divinely.

We were all born young, weren't we? And in our hearts, we all want to stay that way. We *can* stay that way.

In order that we may learn to understand and cooperate with the infinite urge and ardor of God's life within us, which wants to live and live and keep on living, let us practice and pray our way, every day, into our predestined divine condition: youthful maturity, the true goal of life.

# Chapter X

*How to Keep Your Body in Good Running Order*

Many of us want to stay young in mind and body. In order to be effective, our desire has to be translated into action, intelligent action. We should seek to understand what our body needs to function at its best for us. Then we should make up our mind to give our body whatever it requires, to care for it even better than we care for our car.

For it is probably safe to say that if we treated our car as casually as many of us treat our body, we would soon have car trouble! And it would serve us right. Fortunately, where cars are concerned, the service stations keep reminding us of their needs, and checking to see that those needs are supplied. Even the most unthinking driver gives his car the minimum of care needed to keep it in good running order.

It is also probably safe to say that our mental attitude toward our car is based on the fact that it cost us money. Having paid our good money for it, we want to get our money's worth out of it.

This attitude does not apply to our physical body. We have had a physical body ever since we can remember. We never paid anything for it, so we take it for granted, as we do the majority of the good things in life. But suppose you had paid for your body. Suppose it had cost you a million dollars. How would you be treating it right now?

Another question: Can you buy a living, functioning human body, such as yours, and be able to live in it, even for a million dollars?

Then how much is the body worth that you have right now?

Since you cannot get another one at any price, your present body is priceless, isn't it?

You have a body that could not be replaced for all the wealth on Wall Street. How well are you taking care of this priceless body of yours? How much do you know about its needs? Are you just taking everything about your invaluable body for granted, just letting it take care of itself? You may be thinking: "Why not? Why shouldn't I take its performance for granted? Everybody else does."

But you are not everybody else. You are different. You are progressive. You are interested in living as long as you can, provided you can enjoy life as long as you live. That is why you are reading this book.

Let me give you my ideas of what that "billion-dollar-plus" body of yours needs to keep it in good running order, regardless of passing years. *First,* good health depends on understanding your body's needs, and caring for them intelligently. *Second,* you must understand the needs of your mind, and care for them. (I have dealt at some length with the needs of your mind, particularly its need for consciously directed renewal, also the need for constant exercise of the mental faculties by studying and learning new things, in Chapters IV and V.)

But above all, there is a spiritual factor in continued good health. I believe that continued good health depends on understanding your own deep, inner relationship to the spiritual Source of life within you. For is it not the divine life force within your body that really keeps it alive and well?

Does this sound too religious, or too deep, or too "spooky" to be practical? It is not a bit more mysterious than putting distilled water in the battery of your car . . . and it is just as practical. Few of us can explain the chemical process by which distilled water keeps a car battery alive, and in fact the whole construction and operation of a battery is a mystery to us. But that does not prevent us from keeping that battery supplied with what it needs to keep the car in good running order. We take the word of others who know more about the matter; that is good common sense.

I hope that you will be just as practical in your approach to understanding the needs of your body and your mind, and the role of your inner spiritual organism, so that you can do your part in supplying their needs. The wisest men of science do not know everything about the human body. But that does not prevent them from sharing with us what they have learned and what they do know about the body and the mind. They have found that certain things work, therefore they recommend and use them.

There is today a great store of information on the proper care of the body, available for anyone who desires it. Authorities on nutrition, on medicine, on the part the mind plays in keeping the body well, on exercise and recreation, have given of their knowledge and experience.

If we are sufficiently motivated to understand and care for the needs of our mind and body, we can do it. Yes, we can, if we choose, live long and stay vital and energetic. But as a rule this will demand some extra effort and discipline from us. We should be ready, if need be, to give up some of our customary living habits in order to enjoy good health. Many of the average person's habits are founded on nothing more than custom, erroneous beliefs, even superstition. Such habits are not good enough for one who wants to live in this new way and enjoy what the doctors now call "positive health." With the resources of up-to-date information available, all we really need is enough "want to," then we shall become well informed on what this one and only body of ours needs to live in new, youth-giving ways.

Yet for the finest results, we shall need a kind of inward monitor, a secret wisdom, to help us combine all this information and use it intelligently, in the way that will meet our own particular needs at any given time.

Just imagine what it would be like always to have instantly available to you the advice and instruction of someone who was an expert on all these different ways of caring for your body and giving it just what it needed. Well, you do have such a source of guidance available to you. It is right in the depths of your own inner nature at this moment.

But this marvelous inner intelligence is seldom known to the average person. He is familiar with only one phase, one level of his mental equipment: the intellect, or conscious mind. He sometimes has hunches, intuitions, unexplainable flashes of knowledge, sometimes indicating the future. He does not know that such things are the product of this same intelligence we are talking about, the "superconscious mind," which transcends in wisdom and power anything dreamed of by his human intellect.

All that is required for us to become more aware

of this superconscious intelligence and come in tune with it, is our believing that it is within us, that it is deeply interested in our welfare, and our seeking for its guidance. It is on our side. It knows all the answers. It wants *us* to know the answers. In fact, it is devoted to our well-being, safety, and self-preservation!

Again, although this may sound mysterious and "occult," it is not. For the wondrous power that formed your body before it was born is infinitely wise and superlatively knowing; you and I cannot even imagine its wealth of knowledge. After we examine the wonders that life performs in the world of nature, where it is the builder of all living forms, our wonder grows. The body of even a tiny, fragile insect, when examined under a powerful microscope, is a miracle of ingenuity and power. Obviously it has been planned and constructed with as much care as is lavished on the body of the highest type of animal.

Such infinite care and solicitude can mean only one thing: the Power that makes these things loves them. The body of the tiniest midge, as well as the body of man, is a labor of love.

As further proof that all living things are beloved, some sort of provision is always made for their needs. Many are provided with means of self-defense or protection. This, to me, argues that life, or the Power responsible for making these things, sustains them and seeks to care for them. Can we not argue that it is a loving Power which gives life to them, and to us, and to all things?

If you will ponder on this thought that there is a wonderful Superintelligence which is the source of the life in your mind, and also think about the loving nature of this Intelligence, you will begin to have faith that it formed you and loves to care for you in every way. Never think of the life force in your body as being mechanical in nature. Do not think of it as belonging to the world of matter, either. Cultivate the idea that the life in your mind and body is spiritual; it derives from God, and God is infinite love and wisdom.

Besides thinking of the life in yourself as divinely intelligent and loving, think of life as constructive in nature. Life has to be constructive in order to build the innumerable varieties of bodies and structures required by all its myriad expressions on the earth. Being constructive, driven by its very nature and ability always to build, to maintain, progress, advance, and improve, *life is always in favor of more life.* Also, life is in favor of more strength, more energy, more beauty, more physical grace and freedom. Life loves to increase livingness in anyone who knows how to give it the opportunity.

Naturally, life is always in favor of preserving and maintaining itself by renewing and bettering itself. It loves to grow, to be in action, to expand. It springs instantly into action to defend, protect, rescue, and heal any part of itself.

If we can remember this, we will not be so fearful of germs or viruses or infections which we are urged to believe are always trying to invade us. Life is not in favor of viruses or germs, if they are destructive. It will always battle and seek to destroy such invaders, because life is in favor of good health. From the absolute standpoint, life force cannot be diseased, for it is the nature of divine life to renew and purify itself constantly.

Life cannot be in favor of old age, if by age we mean feebleness, stiffness, infirmity, and loss of power to live. By its very nature, life is always in favor of more livingness, of continued livingness; perhaps (as some of us think) life is even in favor of living forever!

Being constructive by nature, life is in favor of youthfulness, freshness, flexibility, vigor, and energy, because these express life. Life responds quickly to wholesome, constructive activity. Perhaps there is nothing that encourages us quite so much as seeing how quickly our body responds to regular physical exercise by becoming more youthful and energetic. The tissues of the body will soon change their appearance. They will firm up and impart a freshness and tone to the skin, which of course will banish wrinkles.

The muscles will shed unsightly fat and become more rounded, well defined and springy. Joints and muscles will become more flexible. What a feedback of happiness we feel now! This is not vanity; it is increased self-respect. We all crave this kind of natural happiness. Sometimes we try desperately to obtain it by unnatural or wrong methods. For example, when the body doesn't get the exercise it needs, it causes a craving in us. This is actually a hunger of our muscles for exercise and activity. Not knowing its real nature, many people react to this muscle hunger by giving the body more food to quiet its cravings, until gradually there isn't much "talk" coming to them from their body. They have overstuffed it with food and dulled it with drink or stimulants, so that the body tone is dulled by weakness and fat. How tragic to do this, when the quiet, satisfying happiness we really crave can be ours for the price of a little effort!

Fortunately the body, which will condition itself so easily and quickly to almost any mode of living, will recondition itself just as quickly to a new pattern if given the opportunity. For instance, if you have not been taking regular exercise, your body is conditioned to not exercising, to being inactive in this respect. It may be soft and relatively weak. It will protest at first when you do start to exercise. The thought may occur to you that it is difficult or even risky for you to exercise. Your subconscious mind may react with fear to any unusual exertion, because it has been conditioned to physical inactivity.

Of course it is necessary for you to use good judgment and not overdo in any way. Think of the wisdom of your superconscious mind, supervising your efforts, restraining you if necessary, inspiring you if needed. Your body is so highly adaptable that it will quickly recondition itself to exercise and activity. You will gain more energy. As your energy increases you will find it natural to be more active and energetic. You will walk more, and walk more briskly. You will be on your feet more and sit less. Soon your body will be conditioned to brisk movements, activity, energetic action, and enjoyment of life. Try this, and see how easy it is to condition your body to be more youthful through exercise.

The very adaptability of our body and mind, the way they condition themselves often without our knowing that they are doing so, can be our greatest ally in progress toward any desired end, provided we use this principle of conditioning by consciously directed thinking and activity.

I once lived in a men's dormitory. One of the front steps had developed a hollow in it. The hollow was filled in with cement, and boards were placed over the step until the cement hardened. After the boards were removed I sensed that my foot felt something was wrong with the step. It was feeling for the hollow which it had been conditioned to find there, and to which it had adjusted. This feeling of strangeness persisted for several days, then my foot adjusted to the new, smooth step. It was reconditioned to a smooth step, without a hollow.

People can become accustomed to abnormal ways of living, adjust subconsciously to them, and feel lost when these abnormal conditions are removed. A friend had been under constant stress due to the prolonged illness of a loved one. After her loved one's passing, she did not react at all as she had expected to do. Instead of feeling free at last from the stress and strain, she felt almost as if she were the one who had died. She had conditioned herself so subtly to the strain and sorrow during the long illness that now she did not know herself. She found herself alone with a new self, unfamiliar, lost. The period of adjustment was trying. For a time she wanted only quiet and seclusion. Books and meditations which had meant so much now seemed empty. But as I write, she has emerged to some extent from the experience, feeling that she is a stronger person, knowing better than ever before "who she is," and determined to be herself, not just to react to the actions of other people.

It is fortunate for us that life is constructive. The

sheer constructiveness of life will always pick us up, even out of the depths, if we are patient, refuse to get panicky, and work with our inner Self during any period of reconditioning. Let us remind ourself over and over: *Life is constructive. Life has a divine idea of the divine way for me to live and to be. Life is working in me right now to bring this divine idea into shape, into form.*

We can trust life. To quote Ella Pomeroy: "Life takes shape. It builds for itself a house, a form, it makes itself manifest. The history of an intelligent human life is the story of an inner stream of activity seeking to win to itself the type and style of form that will best express itself."

Charles Fillmore delighted in studying and meditating on the true nature of the life force that animates us. He was constantly seeking to express God's life in greater measure. In his great book *The Twelve Powers of Man,* Mr. Fillmore said, "Life is the energy that propels all forms to action."

Since we know that all material things are composed of units of electrical energy in a state of high incessant activity, it seems clear that life demands activity of some kind as a condition of its continued expression.

Which brings up again the importance of maintaining physical activity in order to keep young. The physicians who study the aging process strongly recommend regular physical exercise for people of all ages who wish to stay in good health. In the American Medical Association booklet, "A New Concept of Aging," Dr. F. J. L. Blasingame, speaking of exercise, says, "From Dr. Paul Dudley White, for example, it was learned that regular exercise can be a potent defense against deterioration at any age, and there is no such thing as an age when exercise should be stopped."

And Dr. Frederick C. Swartz, chairman of the Committee on Aging, American Medical Association, has been quoted as saying, "The life expectancy figure should jump ten years in one generation if Americans—along with enjoying the medical advances of our time—would exert some degree of self-discipline in practicing daily mental and physical exercise."

What form of exercise does he recommend? He says the best daily exercise he has seen is the Royal Canadian Air Force series, which takes only eleven minutes. But, he points out, he does not regard as exercise such things as golf, bowling, or even housework, because people do not exert themselves enough. Walking, he says, is fine exercise but most people, especially women, don't really know how to walk; they just shuffle along.

Larry Lewis, who is enthusiastic about the value of running, and maintains his remarkable physical fitness at the age of 101 by running more than six miles every morning, recommends walking as the best way for anyone to start conditioning himself. If you are not used to walking, he says, you should start out by walking a few blocks a day at first. As you gain strength, walk another block or two, till you are walking a mile easily every day. If you want to jog, start to jog one block out of your mile walk, then two blocks, and so on. In this way, you will gradually build up your endurance, and soon you will not want to limit yourself to one mile, but will increase the distance you walk or jog, without forcing yourself. Of course, says Lewis, if you doubt your physical soundness, check with a physician before you attempt any form of physical exercise.

How easy it is to convince ourself of the value of physical exercise! We are all in favor of exercise in theory, or as the diplomatic people say, "in principle." It is usually much more difficult to make ourself get up out of an easy chair and actually do our exercises regularly. This takes motivation.

Even such a sturdy character as Benjamin Franklin, although he wrote forcefully of the value of walking and using one's legs, apparently suffered at times from "motivational fatigue," which caused him to find easy and highly rational excuses for avoiding the use of his legs.

In his amusing "Dialogue with the Gout," an imaginary argument carried on at midnight when Franklin was being kept awake by the sharp pains of gout, he tells how "Madame Gout" reproaches him because he has not followed his own advice to go walking in the morning, but has made a variety of excuses instead. Franklin says airily, "Oh, that may have happened ten times in a year." To which Madame Gout pointedly replies: "Your confession is not anywhere near the truth. The actual amount is nearer two hundred times."

Of course we all know how true it is that a tendency to skip our exercise period or to avoid physical effort altogether is strengthened with every evasion of effort. Whereas every little bit of exercise makes it easier to take more exercise. Let me jot down a few incentives to exercise:

Don't be just a wishy-washy "Wish-I-coulder"! Get up off the end of your spine. It's had far too much exercise already. *Do your exercises!*

Regular physical exercise makes your body feel lighter and younger. Lack of exercise causes it to feel heavy and old.

The easy chair, it is said, has probably killed ten times more people, before their time, than has the automobile.

Do you want to be happier? Then put more happiness into your life. There is a quiet "feedback" of happiness from a body that is properly and regularly exercised. When the body is exercised, circulation is speeded up and tissues renewed. Though the body may protest at first if it has been allowed to stagnate, later it will purr with satisfaction.

Think of your muscles being firm, supple, dynamic, strength-packed, feeding back to you the quiet feeling of happiness and satisfaction that a well-cared-for and exercised body gives you as a reward.

Voluntary exertion in the form of physical exercise is not only beneficial physically, it is also beneficial psychologically. It boosts your self-respect, so it improves your morale. Making yourself do your exercises regularly does give you an increased feeling of self-respect. You feel better not only physically but also mentally. Increased self-respect increases your self-confidence and your satisfaction in living.

Regular exercise periods are like deposits in a "bank of youthfulness." And it is the regularity of your deposits that counts. Have you made a deposit in your "bank of youthfulness" today, by taking exercise? Try putting a gold star on the calendar every day you exercise, or keep a record of some kind. It is a great help, and also an inspiration, to see that you have been faithful.

Long ago I read this maxim by a professional wrestler who had recovered from a broken back and returned to the ring through regular exercise. He said: *"The weaker the body, the more it commands. The stronger the body, the more it obeys."*

Regular exercise and physical activity mean youthful health and freedom of movement. Inactivity, indolence, and avoidance of regular exercise mean stagnation in mind and body, stiffness, fears, overweight, and all the sorrows of age. As Jack LaLanne, the popular television health teacher, says, "What makes tomorrow better is what you have done today."

The most startling incentives to regular physical exercise have been produced by research in the effect of physical inactivity on the human body, done at the University of California at Los Angeles by Dr. Laurence E. Morehouse.* Dr. Morehouse, who is professor of physical education, has been conducting experiments for eighteen years to find out what changes take place in the sedentary man. (I define the sedentary man as one who "sits on the end of his spine, in a more or less upright position, for a very large part of his time.")

As a result of his research, Dr. Morehouse feels that regular physical exercise should be thought of more as *self-preservation* than as self-improvement!

Of course the program that Dr. Morehouse super-

* All material on Dr. Morehouse's experiments used by permission, of Dr. Morehouse, University of California "University Explorer," and CBS.

vises was designed to find out what happens to the human body when inactivity is carried to extremes. "It's like putting sedentary man under a microscope," he says, "for it magnifies the reactions that occur when he is moderately sedentary." Volunteers are subjected to such situations as being buried in sand for several hours, or kept floating in water for two weeks at a time. Some are placed in reclining chairs, with their hands strapped to their sides; others must remain lying down in bed for a month or more. In some cases the confinement is achieved by a plaster cast covering the whole body, the objective being to restrict all movement.

What happens to the human body as a consequence of such restriction of movement? We think first of the changes in muscular tissue, and there are some. But Dr. Morehouse says that immobilization affects body chemistry as well. Coronary blood vessels feeding the heart begin to deteriorate very quickly, and even blood components are altered.

Still more startling are the effects of inactivity on the bones. Most of us probably think of our bones as being fixed, solid, and permanent in their nature. But bones like other parts of the body are alive and subject to change. Lack of physical movement, says Dr. Morehouse, causes bones to become spongy and porous. The density of the bone diminishes and it becomes far more susceptible to fracture. Spontaneous fracture of the hips in older women may be explained by this phenomenon.

Lack of exercise may be a lethal letdown for older people. A rocking chair is no substitute for standing on one's own feet, at least a part of every day. The degenerative changes that Dr. Morehouse has identified in the course of experiments in the Human Performance Laboratory have prompted him to set up guidelines to help the average person prevent these regressions. He has demonstrated that by observing a few simple rules the debilitation that overtook his volunteers after only a few days of physical inactivity can be avoided.

When asked by the "University Explorer" (Hale Sparks) to tell what type of activity he recommends to avoid physical decline, Dr. Morehouse gave as his first guideline, "Stay on your feet for a total of two hours a day, every day."

He urges people who do a great deal of driving or sitting behind a desk to take every opportunity to stand up and walk around. The driver should get out and walk around while the gas tank is being filled. The office worker should stand and stretch during a telephone call. Getting things out of a file increases the time you spend on your feet. Being on the feet for a couple of hours a day keeps the bones strong by placing them under what Dr. Morehouse calls "longitudinal compression."

He has proved that to maintain healthy bones one must subject them to frequent shock and strain. There is laboratory proof that vertical stress from standing is essential to physical fitness. Persons who do not spend much time on their feet have a tendency to faint easily, because blood tends to collect in their legs when they do rise and blood pressure tends to drop in the heart and brain. In the long run, then, the housewife who spends several hours a day at the stove, the sink, and the end of a broom can take consolation in the fact that her proper quota of longitudinal compression is built into her job!

Another important physiological requirement is to raise the heartbeat rate to 120 beats per minute for a period of from one to three minutes, every day. Dr. Morehouse says this can be accomplished by any exercise strenuous enough to make you feel your heart pounding in your chest. If you begin to feel a pounding in your temples, however, it means you are overexerting yourself.

According to Dr. Morehouse, hurrying up a flight of stairs two steps at a time will usually accelerate your heart to 120 beats per minute, as will carrying a big load of groceries, laundry, or rubbish. Individuals who do not exert themselves in some manner to step up their heart rate are allowing it to degenerate. Without this periodic step-up the size of the heart muscle actually decreases. The blood vessels feeding the heart deteriorate, cutting down coronary circulation. These regressions eventually cause the heart to pound heavily after the slightest exertion, and in time might even lead to biochemical failure of the heart.

If you want to reduce, here is another startling discovery made by Dr. Morehouse: Exercise before eating actually depresses the appetite! Lack of physical activity does not reduce your appetite, it increases it. If you want to eat less, he suggests taking some physical exercise just before eating.

If you accept his dictum that regular exercise is self-preservation, you should use your ingenuity (if you are at all sedentary) to make exercises out of tasks, perhaps to take an exercise break instead of a coffee break. You can walk for exercise in a very small space, if you do it properly.

For instance, on a Canadian Pacific steamer

coming down the Inside Passage on the British Columbia coast, a friend and I watched fascinated as the captain took his "constitutional" in the narrow confines of the ship's bridge. Head erect, shoulders back, hands clasped behind his back, he paced with measured, brisk, emphatic steps across the little space. A few crisp, snappy steps, then about face, forward and back he marched. He explained to us that he could walk several miles a day by this method. I find that if you have a clear space of twenty feet in your office (probably twice what the captain had), if you walk this or jog it fifteen times, you have covered a hundred yards. Try it, several times a day.

Readers of this book will be in such varying degrees of physical fitness that it is inadvisable for me to recommend even mild exercise for everyone. You must be the judge of what you can do in this respect. If you are unaccustomed to exercise, or have any doubts about your physical condition, check with your physician. All recommendations made here concerning exercise are for those in good health, or those who are assured that they are capable of exercising without harm. If you are capable of exercise, you can choose some sort of program for yourself and keep at it, with the resulting exhilaration and improved physical fitness that will result as your reward.

I notice that regularity in taking exercise counts. After only three days of exercising regularly instead of occasionally, I began to feel the benefits. Already I was more flexible, and had more endurance. I began to feel this "feedback" of quiet happiness and sense of well-being from my body. Five days of

regular exercise was even better. On about the
seventh day I had occasion to run for my bus: no
breathlessness . . . I did it easily.

Don't complain if you have to be on your feet.
Think how good it is for your bones and your heart
and your muscles.

If you are sedentary find opportunities to stand as
often as you can. Learn stretching exercises and do
them. There are now paperback books available
giving instructions and motivation for every type of
exercise—the milder yoga types, the stretching
types, the exercise-by-posture, the more vigorous
forms such as the Royal Canadian Air Force series
already mentioned, aerobics, and others.

The one basic thought to remember is: *If you
want to live longer and stay younger, regular physical activity is a "must."*

In our cultivation of youthful maturity, in gaining
the pep and drive of youth with the judicious moderation of maturity, neither exercise alone, nor diet
alone, nor metaphysics and right thinking alone will
give us the total effect. We need a judicious combination of all these, plus exercise of the mind, in the
form of studying something new. And lastly, we
need to provide for the needs of the great hidden
spiritual side of our nature, through some form of
religion. I have read that Larry Lewis, after taking his
morning run, has a nap and then goes to a Bible study
class.

You can of course exist for a certain length of
time without doing these things. But can you really
*live,* as you want to live, at peak enjoyment of life,
without them?

# Chapter XI

*Meditation and Eternal Values*

The word *meditation* speaks of a practice that is at once an art, a science, and an instant education. There is a spiritual tradition that in ancient times, when life was more simple, less complicated, and less hurried than it is for most of us today, meditation was practiced on a wide scale by young and old, rich and poor, learned and unlearned alike. Since the people had few books, or none, and the repositories of knowledge gained in the past were in men's memory, communicated verbally to one another, naturally people were accustomed to the idea of knowledge being contained and stored in the mind, not in books or written words.

Since mind was man's own possession, he quite properly felt that the knowledge he needed was already in his own mind, and it required only the practice of certain modes of mind action, known as meditation, to uncover or bring forward the desired knowledge and make it consciously his. This accounts in part for the widespread use of meditation in ancient times.

Today, deluged as we are by printed words, bombarded by visual stimuli through television and movies, deafened by the barrage of radio programs, dulled by the monotonously soothing background music so common in the commercial world, we are too busy coping (or trying to cope) with the responses of our senses to do much more than merely

react to them. We are kept so busy in thus reacting to
the demands made upon our mind by the overstimu-
lated activity of our senses that pure thought, mental
activity for the sake and pleasure of mental activity,
is almost impossible. We consider ourself fortunate if
we can sit down quietly and read a book once in a
while.

But even here, we are depending on our visual
sense for the stimulation of mental activity. We are
not pleasantly and profitably engaged in mental
activity which is concerned only with mental activity itself, with thinking suggested by thinking, with
the necessary flow of ideas resulting from the
impinging of other ideas upon our mind. No, we are
following a prescribed pattern of thought coming to
us from outside of ourself, and incited in the first
place by the stimulation of our eyeballs and optic
nerves. This is not to say that the reading of books
should be discontinued.

But meditation, pleasant and profitable mental
activity originating in self-chosen mental activity
and the free play of interaction of idea and attention
to those ideas, is even more necessary and beneficial
to the mind than the best reading matter can be. We
must revive the lost art of meditation. The knowledge of it still exists in the great racial subconscious
which is available to us all. We can, by wisely directed and skillful persistence, recover from this
great and arcane storehouse of secrets, known as the
racial supermind, the knowledge of how to meditate
effectively, fruitfully, and happily. And we shall
thereby regain much of what we have lost from our
own soul. To begin, an attitude such as this is helpful:

*I praise God for showing me how to meditate
effectively, fruitfully, and happily.*

How shall we meditate? And upon what subject
will our mind be centered during this time? The subject we choose to meditate upon is of the first order
of importance, not the way in which we do it. The
way in which we shall meditate, the techniques (if
there are any generally agreed upon), will be given to
us in proportion as we choose subjects for meditation that are in keeping with what we are seeking to
contact.

What we are seeking to contact by this use of our
mind is the vast, serene, imperturbable Source of
everything that has form. It is called by some the
Oversoul. Emerson wrote eloquently of the Oversoul
because in long periods of silent meditation upon
certain eternal verities he had touched the great im-
personal Mind, or soul of the universe, and he was
moved to tell of its marked contrast to the feverish,
scheming human intellect, which is the only form of
intelligence known to many of us. A helpful affirmation would be:

*Divine wisdom guides me in my choice of an
object for meditation.*

We gain a valuable clue to the correct practice of
meditation. We must choose for our object of meditation something that is eternally true. True, that is,
in the majestic higher sense of that word, which
really means "sustaining an exact perpendicular to
its source." That which is true, in the case of a physical thing or structure standing upright on the earth's
surface, must have its center of gravity in exact
perpendicular to its source of equilibrium.

In building a house, for instance, the building site

must first be made level, and the foundation also must be level, at right angles to the walls it is to support. Everything must be "trued" in its "right" angle to the gravitational force. Otherwise the ceaseless tug of gravitational force will in time pull it down to earth. But if the foundation of the structure is level, and the uprights are truly upright, their right relation to their center of gravity then becomes an anchoring or sustaining force. Such were the principles worked out by ancient builders, who intuitively knew what "true" meant, in building a house or a temple.

But how shall we know what is true in choosing a subject for meditation? Why not choose the word *true* itself as a subject? Before attempting to meditate on this (or any subject) we must bring our mind into what might be called the meditative state. So let us proceed with the necessary steps in our mental preparation before we consider the word *true* any further. We shall return to it as soon as we have established the mood of meditation. Now for the first step in preparation.

We know that meditation is a certain kind of thought. It is calm thought, unhurried thought. Its object is to feel toward, to extend mental fingers toward, the soul of things. And the soul of things is infinitely unhurried, absolutely serene. It has to be.

If the source, the realm of cause, was hurried, it would be lacking in efficiency, because it was lacking in the time necessary to do properly that which was to be done. This is unthinkable—that an infinite Source, being infinite, could also be finite, that is, limited or lacking in some way. The two are mutually contradictory. The Infinite cannot lack anything. It cannot lack time, therefore it cannot be hurried.

Thus he who would contact the Infinite must first clear from his mind the sense of hurry, rush, fear, impatience, and lack which so plagues the human intellect. Let us make an affirmation for this purpose: *I clear from my mind all sense of hurry, rush, fear, impatience, or lack.*

In other words, the first thing to do in meditation is to assume the mood of meditation: *I now assume the mood of meditation, which is peace, calmness, serenity.*

How do we assume this mood? We choose to assume it, because we have the power to do so: *I turn my thoughts to the idea of being calm, of being serene, of being at peace. I mentally feel for peace.*

We can feel for peace mentally. Each of us has known what it means to be at peace in our own mind. We think of this memory, choosing quietly, serenely to be at peace: *I choose quietly, serenely, to be at peace.*

We make no effort. If our feelings are upset, in a turmoil, if we are tense from effort or anxiety, no matter. In fact, this sometimes makes it all the easier to choose peace. The mind can make an about face, a reverse, very easily. It can swing abruptly from tumult to peace, if the idea is calmly and persistently held before it of suddenly being at peace.

So we choose peace, but not in a belligerent attitude toward our enemies, the thoughts that are opposing it. They have no choice but to be as they are, because we gave them their character when we indulged ourself in thinking them. Why should we fight them? Why should we resist or resent them?

They are only mistaken consequences of our own thought power. We turn from them and choose calmly to create the mood of peace, the mood of meditation. How delightful it is even to try to think of peace, of being serenely one with the higher world!

This is what peace is. It is being one with the higher world, the world which rules, which is always calm because it is always in command. Why should it not be calm? Can anything external to it challenge its authority? Can you imagine any power which would upset or prevent the majestic order of the stars in their comings and goings?

Well, then, neither can you imagine any power in the feverish, hurried, impatient little intellect to dethrone the majestic peace of the higher world in you. Yes, there is a higher world in you. If there were not, there would be no you, because there would be no center to sustain you in right relation to your cosmic source. Let us sum up what we have said here, in affirmative form:

*I choose quietly, serenely, to be at peace.*

*I turn from any sense of contention and choose calmly to create the mood of peace, the mood of meditation.*

*How delightful it is to think of being at peace, of being serenely at one with the higher world, the soul of things!*

Choosing to enter the timeless mood of meditation, in a calm, unhurried way, we find to our delight that this makes it easy for us to be at peace. The calmer and more quiet we can be, the sooner we shall feel in touch with the higher world within ourself, which is ever beneficent toward its offspring, conscious man. Let us realize that we have done this:

*I am one in thought with the higher world which rules, which is always calm.*

*Nothing can disturb the majestic peace of the higher world in me.*

*I choose to enter the timeless world of meditation in a calm, unhurried way. This makes it easy for me to be at peace.*

Having become calm, having slowed down, breathing more slowly and easily, forgetting all sense of effort, we ask our conscious mind to cooperate with us in meditating on the word *true*. Both the conscious and subconscious mind are always eager to cooperate with us, if we only treat them gently and reassuringly. They like games. They like fun. They will undertake almost any task we ask of them and do it perfectly, if we present it to them as a game, as fun, as something to enjoy which also benefits us.

For this reason, no one should ever strain at meditation, or force himself gloomily and tragically to "concentrate." The conscious and subconscious minds are not slaves. They do not like being coerced. They like being asked, persuaded, enticed even, into doing what you want them to do, in a spirit of fun.

Gently ask your conscious mind to cooperate with you in this splendid game of meditating on the word *true*. Tell it that there is a prize for meditating in this way. It will like the prize. It likes to win things just as much as you do.

So together you and your conscious mind are going to win the prize of knowing what this great secret is that lies hidden in the word *true*. Quietly think about it together. If you like, think about its primary meaning of sustaining an exact perpendicular to its source. Think of how much easier it is for you to walk upright than with your body stooped or bent over. You see, your body knows this secret of being true, in the sense of being upright.

As soon as your conscious mind seems to lose interest in the word, ask your subconscious mind to help you, and take up the game of meditation on the word *true*. Perhaps we get the idea: "That is true which not only maintains an exact perpendicular to its source, but rightly represents its source."

For instance, if we were looking at a red rose, and we said, "I am looking at a white rose," that statement would not be true, because the source of the statement was our looking at the red rose, and the statement did not rightly represent its source. It misrepresented it. It was an *untrue* statement.

A man who lies makes a statement which he knows misrepresents what is true. So in the particular degree to which he is lying, he is putting himself out of "true" with the real state of things. Therefore he is bound to suffer for it in some way. We are sure to lose respect for him if we find him in a lie. Why is this? Because of our inherent respect for what is true. To be true, to tell the truth, is of such tremendous importance because a lie instantly reveals a lack of some kind in us. We speak of a lie as a falsehood. The word *false* comes from a word meaning "to deceive." And to deceive inherently carries the meaning of "to take from." The one who lies to you or deceives you takes from you your right to know the truth.

So the liar is a thief, is he not? This is what makes lying so repugnant to us and robs the liar of our respect. He is a thief. And stealing violates the great sovereign law of the universe, the law of balance, or compensation, about which Emerson wrote so forcefully.

See what just a little meditation on the word *true* has revealed! To be sure, we started out with the basic idea that "true" meant sustaining a perpendicular or upright relationship with one's source. And the word *right* originally meant straight, not crooked. Upright means honest. The liar is not honest. He is not properly representing his source. "Up" primarily represents a direction away from the center of gravity—that is, away from the earth. To be upright means to sustain a perpendicular with the source or center of gravity. And the upright man is one who is in balance or in equilibrium with this great law of balance or compensation. He does not knowingly lie or cheat or steal in any way, because that would be untrue to his source, to his nature.

Perhaps the ancients meditated much on this word *true,* or on similar words, and thus established the fundamental concepts of truth, honesty, and justice which are all that hold the house of civilization together. Who can build a house on a foundation that is not true? A certain great nation boasted that it would build a civilization that would last a thousand years on a foundation of "big" lies, injustice, hate, and violation of all moral codes. Instead of lasting a thousand years, it lasted barely twelve years! The savage, unending warfare of universal forces against all that is not true pulled it down in ruins, and its founders with it.

Whatever is not true enters into a losing conflict with all the powerful, unremitting, ceaseless forces that automatically set out to correct or destroy anything not in right relation to its source.

So meditation on the word *true* has brought us face to face with such eternal values as honesty, uprightness, honor, and justice. It has also educated us, if we were not familiar with the great values connected with such abstractions as honesty or truth. We acted scientifically because we proceeded in our mental quest for meaning along exact principles. That is, we followed the principle of beginning our meditation by assuming the mood of meditation, and then we followed the rule or principle of asking the cooperation of our conscious and subconscious minds, instead of trying to force them into action.

But the element of art also entered in. The root of "art," *ar,* meaning to join, also implies the use of skill and power to produce a desired end. So art originally was the skill and power to produce a desired end; it meant the use of the human arms with skill. Nowadays art is defined as knowledge made efficient by skill.

We gained knowledge of the word *true* by enlisting the thinking skill of the conscious and subconscious minds. This made our meditation an art.

Now we have illustrated meditation as a process and a technique which can be followed and mastered by anybody who is willing to make the effort, and will devote the necessary time for this purpose. However, it should also be stressed that one must assume the harmonious, peaceful frame of mind necessary for meditation, to meditate on things that are true, or harmonious with truth.

One does not waste his time and energy thinking of deceit, loss, or personal matters in this kind of meditation. He chooses for his subject words connected with eternal values. Words such as *love, wisdom, beauty, peace, light,* are tremendous subjects for meditation. They induce harmonious thoughts.

Harmony, says Joseph Shipley in his "Dictionary of Word Origins," was originally a term not in music, but in carpentry. It meant "to fit together." He says that both the Greeks and the Indians have a carpenter god. In Christianity, Jesus, the Son of God, was a carpenter. In the beginning, wood was the primary life stuff, of which all things are made. "So it is no historical accident, but a mythical necessity, that the God be referred to as a carpenter."

Harmony usually suggests a pleasing concord of sounds, or of proportions, or of colors. And concord suggests agreement. So harmonious thoughts are thoughts in agreement with the truth or reality of our being. Thoughts which do not clash or conflict with Truth, or with eternal things, are harmonious thoughts.

Thoughts of eternal verities, in harmony with the true state of things in God's world, fit in with the unspoken but potent desires of the soul to be fed with its "bread from heaven," that is, with beautiful ideas from God's world. In its relationship toward God (that of a child to its parents), the soul depends on the invisible world of God's kingdom for its sustenance and nourishment, just as an earthly child depends on its parents for food, clothing, and shelter.

If the human child is not properly fed and cared for, its growth rate suffers, and its well-being declines. If the soul of man, the child of the Eternal, is not properly fed with its own form of nourishment, its growth rate lags and its well-being suffers. The soul's nourishment, as we have mentioned before, is absorbed by it from the higher Self, or "kingdom within," in the form of true, divine ideas. Man's soul has a peculiar empathy with these divine ideas; it welcomes them with fervor, as a nursing child takes the bottle. Being a mental-spiritual organism, the soul feeds on mental elements which embody in their primal meaning fundamental functional ideas, ideas that are part of the mental structure of the universe.

In one sense these are more than ideas, they are principles. We have spoken of the principle of uprightness which governs the right relation of an upright structure, or of a being that walks upright, like man, to the earth's vital forces which hold it in the form of gravitation. It is instructive to note that the principle of uprightness, which governs such structures as houses or tall buildings on the earth's surface, and also governs man's body, can be found in operation as well in the mental and e motional nature of man.

Man must be upright in his dealings with others, or (as we have seen) he begins at once to encounter a corrective tendency, an invisible, nonmechanical force which nevertheless operates with even greater precision than laws of matter. The laws of matter and gravitation contend with a material structure which is out of plumb, that is, out of line with the mechanical principles governing it. In the end, it will topple and fall.

What might be called the moral laws of the universe also contend with those who violate them, and since these laws are timeless and universal in their scope and power, no man or group of men or nation can contend with them for long. Men and women are primarily living souls, who exist as flesh beings by virtue of their connection with an intangible, non-physical world of spiritual principles, ideas, and intangible essences.

This invisible world has its own laws, far more precise and unerring than any law of matter. These laws require exact obedience to their ruling principles, just as do mechanical laws. The soul of humanity intuitively knows this, and tries to obey its spiritual mandates. But the individual soul is often hampered by the mass ignorance of society, and sometimes wastes much of its energy in conforming outwardly to social customs or group morals which it innately knows to be wrong and destructive, while at the same time it resists inwardly such conformance, and reproaches itself for it.

In general the moral principles which have characterized the great, leading religions of the world are much the same. Not harming oneself, not harming one's neighbor, honesty, charity, purity of motive, unselfishness, the giving of full value for value received—these are found in the most ancient religions, as in the Decalogue of Moses.

Yet in our own civilization, which boasts of its advancement, violations of such laws are so widespread that lawlessness almost threatens to become the norm, and lawfulness abnormal. Why should stringent laws be needed to curb the greed of corporations who seek to increase their profits through giving short value for what they receive, in the form of deceitful packaging and short weight? If our thesis is correct, that the universe is opposed to stealing in any form, no one can profit by giving less value for the price than he is supposed to give. Again, why do men risk years of imprisonment to rob banks or stores? They do not know that regardless of whether the state punishes them or not, the higher moral law of the universe is sure to do so, in the long run.

There is no time here to go into the operation of cause and effect, known as karmic law, or to explain its precise and unfailing reward or retribution. But karma is not a "heathen idea." Both Jesus and Paul taught it, although of course Jesus came to show how transgressions of the karmic law could be forgiven by divine grace, if there was true repentance.

The point is, if we want to live effectively we must live not only in harmony with natural laws, but with moral and spiritual law. And, as Marcus Aurelius observed, "The surest path to perfect harmony is to recur to it ever and again." How? Through meditation on harmonious thoughts. We know the rudiments of meditation: the deliberate choice of the meditative mood or frame of mind, the turning of our mind's eye from ugliness, discord, or anything unhappy to the calm delight of thinking about eternal values.

The habit of meditativeness, the ability to place the mind in this condition, is easier to master than you think, because the mind and soul love to engage in this form of mental activity. It is like food and drink to them.

So now we are convinced of the value of cultivating and entertaining harmonious thoughts. This actually nourishes the soul, with its own peculiar form of nourishment. And when the soul is well nourished, the body will be in better health, just as when the body is strong and vigorous we are more optimistic and less inclined to worry about tomorrow. And we have a method of beginning and practicing meditation. But is there any special way to evoke these harmonious thoughts?

The way to call harmonious thoughts into our mind is to think lovingly about them. Think, for instance, how much this word *true* now means to you. You have grasped through meditation something of its high value and its essential force for good in your life. Would you part with this knowledge of what *true* means? No, because you love and value the knowledge.

To summon a similar knowledge of any desired eternal value, you proceed in much the same way. You think with appreciation of what a deeper understanding of its meaning will do for you. It will enrich your life. It will certainly change your mentality for the better, since meditation on worthwhile words is an instantaneous education. So there is a rich prize of value and meaning wrapped up in this word you have selected for contemplation. Think lovingly of it. Look lovingly toward it, in the way you look at someone or something you love. Think: *I would love to know more of the meaning of this word.*

Then ask the cooperation of your conscious and subconscious minds in meditating on it. Immediate results are not always obtained; the mind has its own ways of responding to such efforts. Often in spite of ourself we are exerting pressure, trying to force or coerce the desired unfoldment of meaning into our conscious awareness, instead of happily and lovingly cooperating with the meditative process, letting it deliver.

When we try to coerce or use force, the resulting mental pressure clamps down on the involuntary mental activity that true meditation requires. As a result the delivery of the desired idea or illumination is blocked. Then the subconscious mind will await another time, when the mental tension is off, and a whole train of ideas or feeling will involuntarily occur (perhaps at a most inconvenient time for us; but this is not the fault of the subconscious mind).

It is we ourself who are to blame, because we tried to coerce or force results, instead of lovingly letting them take place. Here is where art has a place in the science of meditation. We learn any art by practice and repeated study. To meditate so as to evoke any desired idea and its meaning into involuntary unfoldment in our mind is indeed an art. We master it by desiring to master it, by learning the letter of it, but even more by obeying the spirit of it.

Remember that in meditation the form is important, the technique is essential, but the spirit in which you seek to use both is vital. Success comes from obeying all three. To blend form, technique, and spirit is indeed a fine art.

You remember that the root meaning of the word *art* was "to join," just as *harmony* means "to fit or blend together." To join, or to fit or blend together with love your conscious effort and the involuntary or spontaneous activity of the higher mental powers in meditation is an art, with its own forms of required discipline, as any devotee of meditation will tell you. But no other art is more richly rewarding, and in fact, no other form of art is so eternally rewarding as meditation. In silent meditation, we fuse into our own character, and even into our soul, values and riches that will last forever.

Perhaps this is one meaning in Jesus' great lesson on building one's house of life upon a rock. There were people in the ancient world who understood this simile perfectly. They were in on the secret of building eternal values into their own character. They knew that character was destiny, and thus man could choose his destiny by choosing his character.

It was the house of consciousness which Jesus urged us to build upon "rock." Rock is firm, unyielding. It suggests a foundation made of substance powerful in its cohesiveness and extremely resistant to external forces. This is a graphic word picture of one who has built his life upon a consciousness of eternal values. How forcefully such a person resists the pressures of the world to conform, when conformity would violate his convictions! He seems to be immune to fear or flattery or base temptation. Can money buy him, or fame turn his head? Of course not, because he has established a value scale within himself. He weighs and tests and measures every idea or possible experience offered to him with his own permanent scale of values.

He is like an assayer, one who tests ores to determine their true content of precious metal. I once went through an Ontario gold mine and talked to the assayer. I was astonished to discover how many minerals that shine and glitter are not gold. All of our party had pieces of rock picked up on the ore dumps; some of them shone like wedding rings, but they were not gold.

The assayer took a piece of rock bigger than a man's fist, with a tiny yellow speck in it at one end, no larger than the head of a pin. "This," he said, "is

gold." Then he showed us how this yellow dot of
metal, no matter how the light fell on it, was always
the same, always reflected the same dull gleam. But
our fool's gold, the glittering pyrites, were bright
from one angle and dull when viewed from another.

The assayer had of course a value scale or system
of tests for determining true gold in his mind. Since
my lump of ore was palpably false by these standards, he smilingly told me that it was worthless. We
can become equally skillful in the all-important
matter of establishing our own value scale. By means
of meditation you and I can become as expert in
judging and selecting the values by which we shall
live as a skilled assayer is in judging ore. Like him, we
shall have in our mind, as a standard for making
judgments, a scale of values based on exact knowledge of exact principles. And this scale of values will
give us unerring insight in the cultivation of the fine
art of selecting our life goals.

These life goals (or values, for the terms are practically synonymous) when tested in the crucible of
experience can turn out to be either worthless fool's
gold, bringing us bitter disappointment, or the
precious metal of eternal values.

# Chapter XII

*Our Values Produce Our Life Goals*

In an earlier period of education in this country, school readers were sure to contain material designed to give the child knowledge of what his elders considered the most valuable and worthwhile things in life, and how to choose them. Take, for instance, Benjamin Franklin's story about the whistle, which stressed the idea of getting full value for one's money.

When he was only seven, with money in his pocket just given to him by relatives, Ben heard the sound of another boy's whistle. Eager to own one, he gave all the coins in his pocket to a shopkeeper for a similar whistle, without even asking its price. He then went proudly home, to show his family what a prize he had for the money.

The family's reaction was prompt. His brothers and sisters and cousins told him he had given four times as much for the whistle as it was worth. They told him what good things he might have had for the rest of the money, and laughed at him so much for his foolishness that at length he cried with chagrin. Thoughts of what he might have bought pained him more than the pleasure he derived from the whistle.

Humiliating as it was at the time, this experience paid dividends as a valuable form of education, since it played a prominent part in establishing Franklin's scale of values. He constantly referred to it in later life; he tells us that many times he kept himself from extravagance by saying, "Now, Ben, don't pay too much for your whistle again!"

From this one incident, Franklin gradually established a scale of values by which he judged the worth of the things most people spend their lives in attaining. Many, many people, he concluded, gave too much for their whistles. He watched his contemporaries seeking favor at court, sacrificing even their friends to attain it, others ruining their business in attaining popularity, some sacrificing everything to accumulate money, and said silently, "You are all paying too much for your whistles."

Finally, as he says in his letter to Madame Brillon, he concluded that most of mankind's miseries were inflicted on them by false estimates they had made of the value of things, hence, "by giving too much for their whistles." They had not educated themselves, as he had, in the art of judging values.

What better gauge of education could there be than the value scale it gives to the student? What sort of a "whistle" is his life going to pay for? Is he going to invest his energy, his time, and his precious years in such perishable things as pleasure, thrills, games, or entertainment? Or is he going in for money, a big car, a fashionable address? Will he sacrifice his health for pleasure, or for advancement in business? Will he sell his honesty and integrity for easy money? Will he drop out of school and take the first job offered at unskilled labor because he values education lightly in comparison with having money of his own? The answers to these questions, and many more, all depend on the value scale the student has been able to establish during his formative years.

Once established, a value scale is hard to change.

Perhaps this is one reason why most religions complain that it is so difficult to change people for the better. We do not really change people; we change the values, the ideas they hold and to which they voluntarily or involuntarily submit every judgment, every decision. "What's in it for me?" speaks of a value scale accustomed to very small measurements, and magnetized around self-interest. The holder of such a value scale things that he is shrewd, that he is "looking after Number One," as the saying is.

But it is not always shrewd to consider one's own convenience, one's own comfort, when there is a call to service, or an opportunity to give of oneself in some way. A newspaper recently carried a story which might have come from an old McGuffey Reader: A woman died, and cut off her nephew, her only heir, with one dollar in her will. She left a total fortune of $957,868 elsewhere. Why? Because when he was a boy her nephew, to quote the newspaper account, "refused to shovel snow, carry out the rubbish barrels, or help her in any way." His value scale evidently led him to refuse to do what his aunt requested, something she evidently considered he should have been glad to do. He lost a fortune as a result.

One could collect many such examples. In a Canadian bank, an old ragpicker was more or less shunned by employees when he came in for his small transactions. No one wanted to look after him, so the manager of the bank always took care of him personally. When the old ragpicker died, it was discovered that he had an estate of fifteen thousand dollars, which he left to the manager. No one suspected that he had that much property. He appeared to be quite poor.

It was only an innate kindness that led the bank official to look after the old ragpicker. He did not want to have the man's feelings hurt. But wasn't this an expression of the official's scale of values? Did he not, wittingly or unwittingly, by his actions show that he valued people for their humanity, and not for their rank on the social scale or their personal appearance?

Like meditation, the wise selection of values by which one lives is a science and also an art. As a rule we select our values or form our scale of values almost unconsciously. Inherited mental attitudes, accepted social standards of our group, prejudices characteristic of our race (acquired or instinctive), all these usually cause us to form our value scale, and then we conform our thinking and our way of living to these standards, without in the least realizing that we are doing so.

But for the one who sets out to practice meditation with any degree of dedication or persistence, such blind and unthinking conformity is no longer possible. He will be touching, tentatively at least, the ancient wisdom that has animated all independent thinkers and spiritual pioneers since history has been recorded. New and startling ideas will occur to him. He will see himself and the values by which he really lives in a new light. He will begin to question them. And he will also look frequently and questioningly, perhaps take what is called "a long, hard look," at the values most generally prized in the society of which he is a part.

This is inevitable. He is opening his mind to instant education through intuitive perception. His dominant thinking must be changed. His values must change. *He* must change. The change will not be dramatic, perhaps, but it will be lasting. It will be the result of real education, inner education if you will, which is the only kind that really counts.

Perhaps the present rebellion on the part of young students is an instinctive reaction to the forced feeding of facts and the cramming of memorized knowledge that has been dominant in our educational system. They want the slower but more lasting method of thinking for themselves, which results in *education by unfoldment from within oneself.* Their instinct is true enough. But since there is seemingly no time and no opportunity for them to be taught in this way, those who can respond to it should be taught a simple method of meditation such as we have been considering. By meditating on the word *intelligence* for even a few moments night and morning, their studies would be much easier and more productive.

Yes, the selection of the values by which we will live is worthy of the status of a fine art. Not only is this true in the sense that the ability to judge wisely and profitably between the many values human existence inevitably offers to us is a very scarce and valuable skill (at least as rare as great artistic talent), but the best means of attaining this good judgment in selecting values is the art of meditation itself!

It seems distinctly possible that the peculiar "sickness" of our society today is just the willingness, even the eagerness, of most people to adopt for their standards of value the things that will reward them the least and harm them the most. Consider the widespread desire for entertainment, and the equally widespread determination to be entertained, diverted, amused, and otherwise emotionally dandled in order to "enjoy oneself." What a world of meaning there is in the term "enjoy yourself"! We seek so much entertainment just because we do *not* enjoy ourself. We do not know how to employ our creative powers of mind and spirit to produce enjoyment for ourself. So there has arisen a great and lucrative industry, the furnishing of entertainment to the masses. So many people can be counted on to watch a popular television show, that a minute of advertising time on this program costs almost a thousand dollars a second!

Entertainment obtained by watching such programs is effortless. It costs nothing in the sense of getting dressed up, or going out to assemble with other people, or paying an admission fee. The cost is all borne by the advertisers. So we have effortless entertainment with the flick of a switch. Yet the question should be asked: Is entertainment itself a true goal or value in life? And even if it is, is *effortless* entertainment a true value? When entertainment is so plentiful and so easily available that one can spend all his leisure hours being entertained with no effort, what effect does this have on his mentality, on his character, on his scale of values?

Is the desire to be entertained, amused, and diverted, to have one's mind kept from thinking, or the desire to have one's attention drawn away from cares and worries arising from one's affairs, a desire that should be gratified without restraint? Granted that we all need some diversion, some means of amusement, is it possible that we are now obtaining diversion and amusement so effortlessly and so indiscriminately and in such quantities that entertainment has stopped fulfilling its original purpose, and has become a major value in life? (To many, these programs are like a habit-forming drug.)

Not only that, but the values expressed in these forms of entertainment are usually of the lowest order, appealing to the most primitive layers of human consciousness. Violence, force, excitement, conflict, all are staple ingredients. It cannot be pretended that the primary purpose of the average television program is to entertain the viewers; the primary purpose is to make sure of great numbers of viewers, in order to justify the vast sums spent by the advertisers for a fleeting moment of each viewer's attention.

This means that primitive emotions must be aroused, in order to guarantee sufficient viewers, and since those in the entertainment industry are industrious students of psychology and human nature, they respond by playing endlessly on such primitive human emotions as fear and sexual desire, which they know to be the dominating motivators on the lower levels of the human psyche.

When you watch your next Western, keep this in mind, and see which of these two basic emotions it appeals to. It will probably be fear. Is not the villain menacing? Doesn't the fear of death or injury (even if it is only injury to someone's ego, or to his self-respect) permeate the action, and lead up to the final, shuddery breath-holding climax? Of course it does.

Now try to answer honestly: Is a half hour or an hour of vicariously experiencing fear, of entertaining fear and even embracing the painful emotion of fear, beneficial to my unconscious mind? Don't I, in my real life, scorn anyone who is unduly fearful; don't I secretly scorn myself for surrendering to fear on occasion? In other words, don't I admire courage, don't I demand it so far as possible in myself and others? Of course you do.

Then if it is courage you want, and courage you admire, how are you going to develop it by practicing being fearful? How are you going to gain more of this supremely desirable quality called courage by saturating your psyche with the emotion of fear, as you do when watching such violence?

But it may be urged: "The hero displays great courage. You are thrilled by your admiration for his courage. You are vicariously experiencing courage by means of identifying with the hero . . . so your vicarious participation in fear is more than offset by identification with courage." Yet is this conclusion sound?

Which is the more common emotion in the show, fear or courage? In order to build up the drama, the fear is intensified as the action develops. And since the tension usually results from a situation where the villain keeps everybody in fear of sudden death, and the development of the plot revolves around the impossibility of dealing effectively with him (regardless of courage), you will probably find that fear predominates for all except a moment or two of the final action. So how much chance do you have to identify with courage?

We still have not answered the question whether entertainment, (if such an exercise in vicarious, painful emotion should be called entertainment) is a desirable end in itself. Is the seeking of entertainment to fill most of the leisure hours of worthwhile value, a desirable goal? Does it contribute to the forming of robust character? Does it strengthen anyone to face and perform his duties and responsibilities? Not when taken in continuing large amounts, or when it is made a chief end in life, we would probably reply. In addition, we should consider the possible effect of overindulgence in fear-arousing "entertainment" on our health.

There is a school of thought which holds that man's subconscious mind cannot distinguish between simulated emotions and real emotions. Do we know whether our subconscious mind can distinguish between vicariously-experienced emotions and real experiences? And what effect does fear have upon the body chemistry? In her book "Let's Get Well," Adelle Davis says, "The stress of anger, fear, keen disappointment, and similar emotions can cause blood fat and cholesterol to soar in minutes."

Studies in psychology show that fear may be learned. That is, the subconscious mind can be conditioned to react automatically to certain situations or to a certain stimulus by being fearful. Are we learning to fear by indulging in vicarious emotions of fear hour after hour, day after day, week after week, month after month, year after year? Does this account for the widespread anxiety which Dr. Arnold Hutschneker, in his book "The Will to Live," says is behind the nameless ailments that cause throngs of people to visit doctors' offices? Many of them he says, are in excellent physical condition. Nevertheless they are sick, sick with hidden fear.

Can we be sure that being instantly and effortlessly entertained by having painful emotions vicari-

ously aroused and experienced has no physical consequences? And even if it can be proved that there
are no physical consequences, how can we know
whether or not there are psychic consequences?
Should we not play safe, and make such dubious
entertainment a very minor part of our life?

Nothing has been said of the "entertainment"
which appeals to the other of the two basic emotions, the sexual urge. Nothing has been said of
anger, another violent and stress-producing emotion.
Blood pressure soars, adrenalin is poured into the
blood by both fear and anger. Considerable evidence
is adduced by Adelle Davis to prove that arthritis is
caused by exhausted adrenals which have been
whipped up for years by violent emotions. Arthritis
is widespread, painful, crippling. If fear and anger
long continued can exhaust the adrenals and so
produce painful, crippling arthritis, does it seem wise
to produce artificially and experience vicariously the
emotions of fear and anger in ourself and call it
entertainment? Is this so-called entertainment really
free? What is it costing us?

In any experience we invest time, as well as the
enormous potential effect of our thought and feeling
upon our mind and body. Actually there is very little
in life that is free. Ben Franklin's little homily about
the whistle is all too true. We pay for everything in
one way or another. And in many cases, there is no
doubt that we pay too much. But there is one thing
in life that really costs us our life: the goals we settle
for as a result of living.

We pay for our goals, or for our values (the words
are practically interchangeable), with our heart's
blood. We invest our life in attaining these goals. Or,

if we are prevented from attaining our goals (or even from pursuing them) as great numbers of people are today by force of circumstances (such as the color of their skin), then we pay in frustration, anger, violent and destructive emotions.

Sydney Harris once said in his column, "Maturity consists, if anything, in knowing the hidden price of whatever you want, and truly judging whether you are willing to pay it." In weighing or considering his scale of values, every person should ask himself, "What am I paying for?" If he can determine fairly well what he is paying for in terms of the investment of his life, then the next question is, "Is it worth it?" In other words, what are the rewards of your goals? Are they worth what you are paying for them?

Sobering thoughts, these, with which to conclude a book bringing an essentially joyous message. For years we have been hearing that a life span of 150 years is just around the corner. And now we have good medical authority for believing that the corner has been turned, that years of themselves need not age the body or cause it to die. Yes, this is indeed a joyous message!

The familiar saying, "Everyone wants to live long, but no one wants to get old," is still true. Now we hold in our hands the knowledge, the spiritual know-how, to make this dream come true. We have the increasing sanction of science to learn how to live without aging; even more, to shed the fear of aging that plagues modern man even in his late youth.

Yet what is the good of prolonging life, of over-coming the aging process, unless we have worthwhile things to do with the added years? What use to discipline ourselves, exercise our body and our mind, retrain our habits of a lifetime, only to pursue the fatuous goals of being amused, of killing time, of killing ourself little by little, as most people do today? Will we go to such lengths to buy longer life, then settle for the least possible values in return? That is not in my scheme of things!

No, the only things worth settling for (that is, paying for) are the eternal things, the eternal values. What are they? The best way to answer that question is to find out for yourself by meditating on eternal values. Only you can decide what are for you the highest values.

The true nature of you, yourself, the true nature of the life force that lives in you, the true nature of the world you inhabit, above all the true nature of the supreme Power behind all things, these are subjects of absorbing and perennial interest. Attainment of a better understanding of any of these vital subjects would be a goal worthy of anyone's best efforts.

It should be clear now that the two terms *meditation* and *eternal values* are related. One is the key to the other. It is by means of the science and art of meditation that we gain an insight into those values (or goals) that have eternal value. They are age-old, and yet imperishable and forever new. Nothing can ever cause such values as honesty, uprightness, justice, truth, wisdom, peace, and unselfish love to be worth less. Every generation finds these things so essential to any really satisfactory mode of living that its members make fresh efforts to possess at least a minimum of these values in their life and in their social systems.

They are also "eternal" in the sense that they are

inexhaustible. Since they are qualities of mind and heart that can be incorporated into our character, our possession of them can be as ageless and lasting as our own soul, which Christians believe to be immortal. Of one of these values the Bible says:

Happy is the man who finds wisdom
and the man who gets understanding
for the gain from it is better than gain from silver
and its profit better than gold.
She is more precious than jewels,
and nothing you desire can compare with her.
Long life is in her right hand;
in her left hand are riches and honor.
Her ways are ways of pleasantness,
and all her paths are peace.
She is a tree of life to those who lay hold of her;
those who hold her fast are called happy.

We need wisdom to guide our love of living aright, above all things. Will the true, vital inner wisdom gained by meditation on eternal values enable us to live longer? I aver that it will. Will this vital wisdom enable us to live better and more fully, as well as longer? After you meditate on it, you can decide for yourself.

Will a day ever come when men will live as long as they please? I think such a day is in the making now. Will you and I live to enjoy that day?

I can speak only for myself. I am working at attaining such a state and such a knowledge right now. In this book I have shared with you much of what I know about the subject. Some of what I know cannot be put into written words as yet, or even communicated verbally. It can be intuitively grasped, however, and felt and lived. You can catch it by thinking of the inspiring examples given in this book, and by collecting your own examples from the news and other sources.

As we study and practice the expression of this wonderful quality of permanent youthfulness, we are sure to have inspiring examples of how well these ideas work. Certainly there must be more for us all to learn about this subject. But in the meantime, in the precious eternal now (which endlessly expands into what we call "time" and "human experience"), let us zealously make the most of the knowledge that we already have. Right now you and I know enough (and to spare) to keep us happily busy, to keep us learning and growing, and so to keep us young.

Of course you are curious (and so am I) about the greater knowledge and acceptance of these ideas which will inevitably develop in this field. But that too is good. Curiosity is a vital element not only in keeping young, but in keeping alive and healthy. Consider the following quotation from "The Menninger Story": "As the doctor recovered, one thing was clear to him: health always depends on the ability to keep one's curiosity alive. There must always be something to look forward to as one goes to sleep at night. Each day must end with at least one question unanswered, one lesson yet to be learned. There must always be things that need one's individual care, whether they be plants or human beings. When he dressed and went to his office again, he was no longer afraid of retirement."*

* Walker Winslow, "The Menninger Story." Gerald Kennedy, A Second Reader's Notebook. New York: Harper and Bros., 1959.

Aren't you curious to see how much of this information you can put to work, and how big a change you will make in yourself by working at it? If you will encourage that curiosity, and work at satisfying it, you will find life so interesting and thrilling and absorbing that you will live and live, and have sheer pleasure doing it!

I think my best word to you is: Never "settle down," in the old sense of the expression. Never say: "This is it. I'm finished; I've only got so many more years to live. I'm going to spend the rest of my life just like this." Anything that settles down sinks, doesn't it? Do you want to be sunk?

Follow the good doctor's example. Always have something going, something to look forward to as you go to sleep at night, even if it is just the golden, life-giving radiations of the sunrise in the morning. Always be learning. Always be studying. Always be determined not to settle for anything but the highest values in life, eternal values.

No matter what changes occur in our society in the coming years, one who lives by eternal values will be open-minded enough and receptive enough to accept the best in what those changes bring. He will never be out of date, or feel lost or out of tune with the times, because he will be in tune with that which is always as new as tomorrow morning: God's ever-renewing life within him.

Now, assuming that you have read this book through, please turn back to the first chapter. There you read, *"Time of itself has no power to age me."* Start knowing the satisfaction of proving that this fundamental premise is true. Then go on to each chapter in turn. Each will give you interesting and vital ideas that you can use and prove for yourself. There is no thrill equal to that of proving these things for yourself.

Remember, there is something in you that is eagerly awaiting demonstration of youth. That something is the life power within you. Do not let worldly doubts or skepticism or the drowsy pull of inertia lead you to disappoint the life power.

Clear your mind right now of foolish fears. Don't listen to the "It's too good to be true" objections. Just begin to cooperate with that marvelous inner livingness that lives through you (to the extent you allow it to do so). Let the infectious youthfulness of God's Spirit fill your whole being, until you return to the springtime of life.

I have saved what is perhaps the most miraculous prayer of all for the last. Take it for your own right now, and dwell on it all through your study of this book. Here is the prayer: *Spirit within me, awaken me to the wonder of myself.*

May the everliving Spirit within you guide, protect, encourage, and direct you, and give you the persistence necessary to find your own youthful maturity.

*Addenda*

### Ever-renewing Youth

I have laid aside the gray old garments of the past;
Since my mind is a mental lung
I now breathe out the false beliefs of age,
And breathe in strength
From the ever-renewing airs of Spirit.

I look forward to something better,
Not backward to something better;
I am still growing, therefore I am young.

I associate myself with the youth of my life-force,
Which is born and renewed with my latest breath;
Therefore I am no older than my latest breath!

I breathe in strength from the in-rolling waves of
      Spirit.
I identify myself with the Spirit and not with its
      outward forms;
Time and change therefore become my allies and
      servants,
Not my masters.

The fictitious record of earthly years
Concerns me no more than it does the tides, or the
      air,
Or the strength of the sun.

The hour and day when my earthly form saw the
      light

Have nothing to do with my enjoyment of life-force.
It is when my mind sees the light that matters!

For I am Spirit. I identify myself with Spirit.
I need not think "I am youth"—
I know it!

*On Finding a Note Dated Several Years Before*

Years are but masks
With which I clothe my thought;
I think a thought and hang it on a peg
And label it as this or that, in time.
The label on the peg is made by me;
It does not make me old or make me young.

That which I am endures as changeless life,
And I can think for endless eons of time
Without its changing me or aging me—
Unless I let my labels frighten me!
Then, through belief, I fear . . .
Because I fear the labels on the pegs
Which I have made!

Shall I bow down before my own conceits?
Shall I believe false concepts of the years,
And fall in fear before my own past thoughts?

No! I am life itself!
I made the labels,
I hung them on the pegs, and numbered them;
Can I not take them off
And tear them up?
I think I will . . .
For so I have the power
To do!

### Meditation for Abundant Life

"He himself gives to all men life and breath
and everything . . . for in him we live and move
and have our being" (Acts 17:25, 28).

Think of life as the silent, harmonious, peaceful
activity of God's physical presence: always creating,
producing, promoting, growing, causing to come
into production, bringing to birth, causing to come
to maturity all of God's perfect ideas that need to be
produced, according to His will.

God is life, abundant, omnipresent, eternal. I am
alive with God.

I am one with this life, abundant, omnipresent,
eternal. I am alive with God.

I have fullness of life now, because I realize that I
live in an energizing sea of abundant, omnipresent,
eternal life. I am alive with God.

I reject, I refuse, I deny the race belief that my life
is limited to threescore years and ten. God is my life,
and God is eternal, unchanging, and abiding. "From
everlasting to everlasting, I change not," says God's
life within me. I am alive with God.

I refuse to entertain any thought of weakness,
sickness, or death. I refuse to believe in old age,
decay, or limitation. In God I live, move, and have
my being, and God is life. I am alive with God.

I think of my life as spiritual, and every faculty
quickens with new life. I am alive with God.

My life will never wane, because I keep in the
consciousness of life as Spirit. I am alive with God.

I think life, I talk life, I see myself filled with the glory of life, and my body shows forth the glory of God. I am alive with God.

I accept in faith now the fact that "the law of the Spirit of life in Christ Jesus hath made me free from the law of sin and death." I am alive with God.

(Based in part on Theodosia DeWitt Schobert's book *Divine Remedies* (Lee's Summit, Mo; (Unity School of Christianity)

PRINTED U.S.A.

106F-15M-11-69